FREE Test Taking Tips DVD Offer

To help us better serve you, we have developed a Test Taking Tips DVD that we would like to give you for FREE. **This DVD covers world-class test taking tips that you can use to be even more successful when you are taking your test.**

All that we ask is that you email us your feedback about your study guide. Please let us know what you thought about it – whether that is good, bad or indifferent.

To get your **FREE Test Taking Tips DVD**, email freedvd@studyguideteam.com with "FREE DVD" in the subject line and the following information in the body of the email:

a. The title of your study guide.

b. Your product rating on a scale of 1-5, with 5 being the highest rating.

c. Your feedback about the study guide. What did you think of it?

d. Your full name and shipping address to send your free DVD.

If you have any questions or concerns, please don't hesitate to contact us at freedvd@studyguideteam.com.

Thanks again!

CLEP College Composition and Modular Study Guide with Practice Test Questions and English Essay Prompts [3rd Edition]

Joshua Rueda

Written and edited by TPB Publishing.

ISBN 13: 9781637751299
ISBN 10: 163775129X

Table of Contents

Quick Overview

As you draw closer to taking your exam, effective preparation becomes more and more important. Thankfully, you have this study guide to help you get ready. Use this guide to help keep your studying on track and refer to it often.

This study guide contains several key sections that will help you be successful on your exam. The guide contains tips for what you should do the night before and the day of the test. Also included are test-taking tips. Knowing the right information is not always enough. Many well-prepared test takers struggle with exams. These tips will help equip you to accurately read, assess, and answer test questions.

A large part of the guide is devoted to showing you what content to expect on the exam and to helping you better understand that content. In this guide are practice test questions so that you can see how well you have grasped the content. Then, answer explanations are provided so that you can understand why you missed certain questions.

Don't try to cram the night before you take your exam. This is not a wise strategy for a few reasons. First, your retention of the information will be low. Your time would be better used by reviewing information you already know rather than trying to learn a lot of new information. Second, you will likely become stressed as you try to gain a large amount of knowledge in a short amount of time. Third, you will be depriving yourself of sleep. So be sure to go to bed at a reasonable time the night before. Being well-rested helps you focus and remain calm.

Be sure to eat a substantial breakfast the morning of the exam. If you are taking the exam in the afternoon, be sure to have a good lunch as well. Being hungry is distracting and can make it difficult to focus. You have hopefully spent lots of time preparing for the exam. Don't let an empty stomach get in the way of success!

When travelling to the testing center, leave earlier than needed. That way, you have a buffer in case you experience any delays. This will help you remain calm and will keep you from missing your appointment time at the testing center.

Be sure to pace yourself during the exam. Don't try to rush through the exam. There is no need to risk performing poorly on the exam just so you can leave the testing center early. Allow yourself to use all of the allotted time if needed.

Remain positive while taking the exam even if you feel like you are performing poorly. Thinking about the content you should have mastered will not help you perform better on the exam.

Once the exam is complete, take some time to relax. Even if you feel that you need to take the exam again, you will be well served by some down time before you begin studying again. It's often easier to convince yourself to study if you know that it will come with a reward!

Test-Taking Strategies

1. Predicting the Answer

When you feel confident in your preparation for a multiple-choice test, try predicting the answer before reading the answer choices. This is especially useful on questions that test objective factual knowledge. By predicting the answer before reading the available choices, you eliminate the possibility that you will be distracted or led astray by an incorrect answer choice. You will feel more confident in your selection if you read the question, predict the answer, and then find your prediction among the answer choices. After using this strategy, be sure to still read all of the answer choices carefully and completely. If you feel unprepared, you should not attempt to predict the answers. This would be a waste of time and an opportunity for your mind to wander in the wrong direction.

2. Reading the Whole Question

Too often, test takers scan a multiple-choice question, recognize a few familiar words, and immediately jump to the answer choices. Test authors are aware of this common impatience, and they will sometimes prey upon it. For instance, a test author might subtly turn the question into a negative, or he or she might redirect the focus of the question right at the end. The only way to avoid falling into these traps is to read the entirety of the question carefully before reading the answer choices.

3. Looking for Wrong Answers

Long and complicated multiple-choice questions can be intimidating. One way to simplify a difficult multiple-choice question is to eliminate all of the answer choices that are clearly wrong. In most sets of answers, there will be at least one selection that can be dismissed right away. If the test is administered on paper, the test taker could draw a line through it to indicate that it may be ignored; otherwise, the test taker will have to perform this operation mentally or on scratch paper. In either case, once the obviously incorrect answers have been eliminated, the remaining choices may be considered. Sometimes identifying the clearly wrong answers will give the test taker some information about the correct answer. For instance, if one of the remaining answer choices is a direct opposite of one of the eliminated answer choices, it may well be the correct answer. The opposite of obviously wrong is obviously right! Of course, this is not always the case. Some answers are obviously incorrect simply because they are irrelevant to the question being asked. Still, identifying and eliminating some incorrect answer choices is a good way to simplify a multiple-choice question.

4. Don't Overanalyze

Anxious test takers often overanalyze questions. When you are nervous, your brain will often run wild, causing you to make associations and discover clues that don't actually exist. If you feel that this may be a problem for you, do whatever you can to slow down during the test. Try taking a deep breath or counting to ten. As you read and consider the question, restrict yourself to the particular words used by the author. Avoid thought tangents about what the author *really* meant, or what he or she was *trying* to say. The only things that matter on a multiple-choice test are the words that are actually in the question. You must avoid reading too much into a multiple-choice question, or supposing that the writer meant something other than what he or she wrote.

5. No Need for Panic

It is wise to learn as many strategies as possible before taking a multiple-choice test, but it is likely that you will come across a few questions for which you simply don't know the answer. In this situation, avoid panicking. Because most multiple-choice tests include dozens of questions, the relative value of a single wrong answer is small. As much as possible, you should compartmentalize each question on a multiple-choice test. In other words, you should not allow your feelings about one question to affect your success on the others. When you find a question that you either don't understand or don't know how to answer, just take a deep breath and do your best. Read the entire question slowly and carefully. Try rephrasing the question a couple of different ways. Then, read all of the answer choices carefully. After eliminating obviously wrong answers, make a selection and move on to the next question.

6. Confusing Answer Choices

When working on a difficult multiple-choice question, there may be a tendency to focus on the answer choices that are the easiest to understand. Many people, whether consciously or not, gravitate to the answer choices that require the least concentration, knowledge, and memory. This is a mistake. When you come across an answer choice that is confusing, you should give it extra attention. A question might be confusing because you do not know the subject matter to which it refers. If this is the case, don't eliminate the answer before you have affirmatively settled on another. When you come across an answer choice of this type, set it aside as you look at the remaining choices. If you can confidently assert that one of the other choices is correct, you can leave the confusing answer aside. Otherwise, you will need to take a moment to try to better understand the confusing answer choice. Rephrasing is one way to tease out the sense of a confusing answer choice.

7. Your First Instinct

Many people struggle with multiple-choice tests because they overthink the questions. If you have studied sufficiently for the test, you should be prepared to trust your first instinct once you have carefully and completely read the question and all of the answer choices. There is a great deal of research suggesting that the mind can come to the correct conclusion very quickly once it has obtained all of the relevant information. At times, it may seem to you as if your intuition is working faster even than your reasoning mind. This may in fact be true. The knowledge you obtain while studying may be retrieved from your subconscious before you have a chance to work out the associations that support it. Verify your instinct by working out the reasons that it should be trusted.

8. Key Words

Many test takers struggle with multiple-choice questions because they have poor reading comprehension skills. Quickly reading and understanding a multiple-choice question requires a mixture of skill and experience. To help with this, try jotting down a few key words and phrases on a piece of scrap paper. Doing this concentrates the process of reading and forces the mind to weigh the relative importance of the question's parts. In selecting words and phrases to write down, the test taker thinks about the question more deeply and carefully. This is especially true for multiple-choice questions that are preceded by a long prompt.

9. Subtle Negatives

One of the oldest tricks in the multiple-choice test writer's book is to subtly reverse the meaning of a question with a word like *not* or *except*. If you are not paying attention to each word in the question, you can easily be led astray by this trick. For instance, a common question format is, "Which of the following is...?" Obviously, if the question instead is, "Which of the following is not...?," then the answer will be quite different. Even worse, the test makers are aware of the potential for this mistake and will include one answer choice that would be correct if the question were not negated or reversed. A test taker who misses the reversal will find what he or she believes to be a correct answer and will be so confident that he or she will fail to reread the question and discover the original error. The only way to avoid this is to practice a wide variety of multiple-choice questions and to pay close attention to each and every word.

10. Reading Every Answer Choice

It may seem obvious, but you should always read every one of the answer choices! Too many test takers fall into the habit of scanning the question and assuming that they understand the question because they recognize a few key words. From there, they pick the first answer choice that answers the question they believe they have read. Test takers who read all of the answer choices might discover that one of the latter answer choices is actually *more* correct. Moreover, reading all of the answer choices can remind you of facts related to the question that can help you arrive at the correct answer. Sometimes, a misstatement or incorrect detail in one of the latter answer choices will trigger your memory of the subject and will enable you to find the right answer. Failing to read all of the answer choices is like not reading all of the items on a restaurant menu: you might miss out on the perfect choice.

11. Spot the Hedges

One of the keys to success on multiple-choice tests is paying close attention to every word. This is never truer than with words like almost, most, some, and sometimes. These words are called "hedges" because they indicate that a statement is not totally true or not true in every place and time. An absolute statement will contain no hedges, but in many subjects, the answers are not always straightforward or absolute. There are always exceptions to the rules in these subjects. For this reason, you should favor those multiple-choice questions that contain hedging language. The presence of qualifying words indicates that the author is taking special care with his or her words, which is certainly important when composing the right answer. After all, there are many ways to be wrong, but there is only one way to be right! For this reason, it is wise to avoid answers that are absolute when taking a multiple-choice test. An absolute answer is one that says things are either all one way or all another. They often include words like *every*, *always*, *best*, and *never*. If you are taking a multiple-choice test in a subject that doesn't lend itself to absolute answers, be on your guard if you see any of these words.

12. Long Answers

In many subject areas, the answers are not simple. As already mentioned, the right answer often requires hedges. Another common feature of the answers to a complex or subjective question are qualifying clauses, which are groups of words that subtly modify the meaning of the sentence. If the question or answer choice describes a rule to which there are exceptions or the subject matter is complicated, ambiguous, or confusing, the correct answer will require many words in order to be expressed clearly and accurately. In essence, you should not be deterred by answer choices that seem excessively long. Oftentimes, the author of the text will not be able to write the correct answer without offering some qualifications and modifications. Your job is to read the answer choices thoroughly and completely and to select the one that most accurately and precisely answers the question.

13. Restating to Understand

Sometimes, a question on a multiple-choice test is difficult not because of what it asks but because of how it is written. If this is the case, restate the question or answer choice in different words. This process serves a couple of important purposes. First, it forces you to concentrate on the core of the question. In order to rephrase the question accurately, you have to understand it well. Rephrasing the question will concentrate your mind on the key words and ideas. Second, it will present the information to your mind in a fresh way. This process may trigger your memory and render some useful scrap of information picked up while studying.

14. True Statements

Sometimes an answer choice will be true in itself, but it does not answer the question. This is one of the main reasons why it is essential to read the question carefully and completely before proceeding to the answer choices. Too often, test takers skip ahead to the answer choices and look for true statements. Having found one of these, they are content to select it without reference to the question above. Obviously, this provides an easy way for test makers to play tricks. The savvy test taker will always read the entire question before turning to the answer choices. Then, having settled on a correct answer choice, he or she will refer to the original question and ensure that the selected answer is relevant. The mistake of choosing a correct-but-irrelevant answer choice is especially common on questions related to specific pieces of objective knowledge. A prepared test taker will have a wealth of factual knowledge at his or her disposal, and should not be careless in its application.

15. No Patterns

One of the more dangerous ideas that circulates about multiple-choice tests is that the correct answers tend to fall into patterns. These erroneous ideas range from a belief that B and C are the most common right answers, to the idea that an unprepared test-taker should answer "A-B-A-C-A-D-A-B-A." It cannot be emphasized enough that pattern-seeking of this type is exactly the WRONG way to approach a multiple-choice test. To begin with, it is highly unlikely that the test maker will plot the correct answers according to some predetermined pattern. The questions are scrambled and delivered in a random order. Furthermore, even if the test maker was following a pattern in the assignation of correct answers, there is no reason why the test taker would know which pattern he or she was using. Any attempt to discern a pattern in the answer choices is a waste of time and a distraction from the real work of taking the test. A test taker would be much better served by extra preparation before the test than by reliance on a pattern in the answers.

FREE DVD OFFER

Don't forget that doing well on your exam includes both understanding the test content and understanding how to use what you know to do well on the test. We offer a completely FREE Test Taking Tips DVD that covers world class test taking tips that you can use to be even more successful when you are taking your test.

All that we ask is that you email us your feedback about your study guide. To get your **FREE Test Taking Tips DVD**, email freedvd@studyguideteam.com with "FREE DVD" in the subject line and the following information in the body of the email:

- The title of your study guide.
- Your product rating on a scale of 1-5, with 5 being the highest rating.
- Your feedback about the study guide. What did you think of it?
- Your full name and shipping address to send your free DVD.

Introduction

Function of the Test

College-Level Examination Program (CLEP) tests are sponsored by College Board. Over 2,900 colleges and universities across the United States and a few outside the U.S. accept passing scores on a CLEP test in lieu of completing one or more of their introductory-level classes. However, not all schools that accept CLEP credit accept every CLEP test for credit. Some accept all thirty-three tests, some accept none, and some fall in between. Scores on CLEP tests are used for few if any purposes aside from the awarding of entry-level college credit. As a result, almost everyone who takes a CLEP test is a current or prospective college student. Many of those test-takers are also members of the U.S. Armed Forces. The federal government pays for tens of thousands of current military members to take CLEP tests, allowing them to obtain college credit without having to take classes that conflict with their military schedules.

There are actually two separate tests for which this study guide is designed—College Composition and College Composition Modular. The two exams both include a multiple-choice section and a writing assessment. The multiple-choice section in each exam is the same, so the only difference is between the writing assessments. The College Composition writing assessment consists of two essays that are graded by College Board. The College Composition Modular essay section will consist of one of the following:

1. The same type of writing assessment as in the College Composition exam but graded by the college or university that the test taker selects

2. A writing assessment developed and scored by the school the test taker selects

3. A totally different assessment designed by the school the test taker selects

It's important to check with the school you attend or plan to attend before taking the exam so that you know their specific requirements.

Test Administration

CLEP tests are offered at thousands of testing centers around the United States, mostly colleges and military bases, as well as some outside the country. Some test centers are only open to a limited group of individuals, usually those who are registered at the institution offering the test.

CLEP tests are internet-based, allowing them to be offered year-round. Test takers seeking a better score may repeat a CLEP test, but no sooner than three months after the initial testing date.

Test takers with a disability may request accommodations at their test center in keeping with the Americans with Disabilities Act. Test takers seeking accommodations should contact their test center well before their test date to find out that center's deadline for requesting and receiving accommodations. Available accommodations include screen magnification, modifiable screen colors, extended time, untimed rest breaks, and use of a reader, amanuensis, or a sign language interpreter.

Test Format

The multiple-choice section consists of fifty multiple-choice items and is allotted fifty minutes. The two essays are allotted seventy minutes combined, unless you are taking the College Composition Modular and your institution is going with option #2 or #3 listed earlier.

The test is intended to measure test takers' understanding of rhetoric and composition, and their ability to apply principles of standard written English. It also covers research and reference skills.

The approximate breakdown of subject matter on the test is as follows:

Subject	**Example topics**	**Percentage**
Conventions of Standard Written English	Syntax, punctuation, agreement, modifiers	10%
Revision Skills	Organization, use of language, transitions, sentence structure	40%
Ability to Use Source Materials	Use of reference materials, evaluation and documentation of sources	25%
Rhetorical Analysis	Tone, rhetorical effects	25%

Scoring

CLEP tests are scored on a scaled score from 20 to 80. The minimum score you can receive and still get credit is a 50-scaled score. However, some institutions set the passing score higher. CLEP tests are pass or fail, so if you meet an institution's minimum score it will appear as a "P" for "Pass" on your transcript. There is no penalty for wrong answers.

Unlike most CLEP tests, the College Composition & College Composition Modular include essays that must be graded by hand. As a result, unlike most CLEP tests, scores are not made available upon completion of the test. Those taking the College Composition exam should receive their scores about two weeks after taking the exam, after essay grading is complete. The essays are scored by college English composition professors on a scale from 1 to 6. The scorers may be provided by the College Board or by the institution administering the exam. These essay scores comprise 50 percent of the total score.

Essay scoring will vary on a school-by-school basis for the College Composition Modular.

Study Prep Plan

1 **Schedule** - Use one of our study schedules below or come up with one of your own.

2 **Relax** - Test anxiety can hurt even the best students. There are many ways to reduce stress. Find the one that works best for you.

3 **Execute** - Once you have a good plan in place, be sure to stick to it.

One Week Study Schedule

Day 1	Conventions of Standard Written English
Day 2	Revision Skills
Day 3	Ability to Use Source Materials
Day 4	The Essays
Day 5	Practice Test
Day 6	First & Second Essay
Day 7	Take Your Exam!

Two Week Study Schedule

Day 1	Conventions of Standard Written English	Day 8	Practice Questions
Day 2	Practice Questions	Day 9	The Essays
Day 3	Revision Skills	Day 10	Practice Test
Day 4	Practice Questions	Day 11	Review Answer Explanations
Day 5	Ability to Use Source Materials	Day 12	First Essay
Day 6	Practice Questions	Day 13	Second Essay
Day 7	Rhetorical Analysis	Day 14	Take Your Exam!

One Month Study Schedule

Day 1	Syntax	Day 11	Sentence Structure	Day 21	Appeals
Day 2	Sentence Boundaries	Day 12	Main Idea, Thesis Statement, and Topic Sentences	Day 22	Rhetorical Effects
Day 3	Concord/Agreement	Day 13	Use of Language	Day 23	Evaluation of Evidence
Day 4	Diction	Day 14	Evaluation of Reasoning	Day 24	Practice Questions
Day 5	Idiom	Day 15	Sentence Level Errors	Day 25	The Essays
Day 6	Punctuation	Day 16	Practice Questions	Day 26	Practice Test
Day 7	Practice Questions	Day 17	Use of Reference Materials	Day 27	Review Answer Explanations
Day 8	Organization	Day 18	Evaluation of Sources	Day 28	First Essay
Day 9	Awareness of Audience, Tone, and Purpose	Day 19	Documentation of Sources	Day 29	Second Essay
Day 10	Level of Detail	Day 20	Practice Questions	Day 30	Take Your Exam!

Conventions of Standard Written English

Syntax

Syntax refers to the arrangement of words, phrases, and clauses to form a sentence. Knowledge of syntax can also give insight into a word's meaning. Here is an example of how the placement of a word can impact its meaning and grammatical function:

A. The development team has reserved the conference room for today.

B. Her quiet and reserved nature is sometimes misinterpreted as unfriendliness when people first meet her.

In addition to using *reserved* to mean different things, each sentence also uses the word to serve a different grammatical function. In sentence A, *reserved* is part of the verb phrase *has reserved,* indicating the meaning "to set aside for a particular use." In sentence B, *reserved* acts as a modifier within the noun phrase "her quiet and reserved nature." Because the word is being used as an adjective to describe a personality characteristic, it calls up a different definition of the word—"restrained or lacking familiarity with others." As this example shows, the function of a word within the overall sentence structure can allude to its meaning. It is also useful to refer to a chart about suffixes and parts of speech as another clue into what grammatical function a word is serving in a sentence.

Parallelism

Parallel structure occurs when phrases or clauses within a sentence contain the same structure. Parallelism increases readability and comprehensibility because it is easy to tell which sentence elements are paired with each other in meaning.

Jennifer enjoys cooking, knitting, and to spend time with her cat.

This sentence is not parallel because the items in the list appear in two different forms. Some are gerunds, which is the verb + ing: *cooking, knitting*. The other item uses the infinitive form, which is to + verb: *to spend*. To create parallelism, all items in the list may reflect the same form:

Jennifer enjoys cooking, knitting, and spending time with her cat.

All of the items in the list are now in gerund forms, so this sentence exhibits parallel structure. Here's another example:

The company is looking for employees who are responsible and with a lot of experience.

Again, the items that are listed in this sentence are not parallel. "Responsible" is an adjective, yet "with a lot of experience" is a prepositional phrase. The sentence elements do not utilize parallel parts of speech.

The company is looking for employees who are responsible and experienced.

"Responsible" and "experienced" are both adjectives, so this sentence now has parallel structure.

Subordination and Coordination

With terms like "coordinate clause" and "subordinating conjunction," grammar terminology can scare people! So, just for a minute, forget about the terms and look at how the sentences work.

Sometimes a sentence has two ideas that work together. For example, say the writer wants to make the following points:

> Seat belt laws have saved an estimated 50,000 lives.
>
> More lives are saved by seat belts every year.

These two ideas are directly related and appear to be of equal importance. Therefore they can be joined with a simple "and" as follows:

> Seat belt laws have saved an estimated 50,000 lives, and more lives are saved by seat belts every year.

The word *and* in the sentence helps the two ideas work together or, in other words, it "coordinates" them. It also serves as a junction where the two ideas come together, better known as a *conjunction*. Therefore, the word *and* is known as a *coordinating conjunction* (a word that helps bring two equal ideas together). Now that the ideas are joined together by a conjunction, they are known as *clauses*. Other coordinating conjunctions include *or*, *but*, and *so*.

Sometimes, however, two ideas in a sentence are *not* of equal importance:

> Seat belt laws have saved an estimated 50,000 lives.
>
> Many more lives could be saved with stronger federal seat belt laws.

In this case, combining the two with a coordinating conjunction (*and*) creates an awkward sentence:

> Seat belt laws have saved an estimated 50,000 lives, and many more lives could be saved with stronger federal seat belt laws.

Now the writer uses a word to show the reader which clause is the most important (or the "boss") of the sentence:

> Although seat belt laws have saved an estimated 50,000 lives, many more lives could be saved with stronger federal seat belt laws.

In this example, the second clause is the key point that the writer wants to make, and the first clause works to set up that point. Since the first clause "works for" the second, it's called the *subordinate clause*. The word *although* tells the reader that this idea isn't as important as the clause that follows. This word is called the *subordinating conjunction*. Other subordinating conjunctions include *after*, *because*, *if*, *since*, *unless*, and many more. As mentioned before, it's easy to spot subordinate clauses because they don't stand on their own (as shown in this previous example):

> Although seat belt laws have saved an estimated 50,000 lives

This is not a complete thought. It needs the other clause (called the *independent clause*) to make sense. On the test, when asked to choose the best subordinating conjunction for a sentence, look at the surrounding text. Choose the word that best allows the sentence to support the writer's argument.

Conjunctions

Conjunctions are vital words that connect words, phrases, thoughts, and ideas. Conjunctions show relationships between components. There are two types: coordinating and subordinating.

Coordinating conjunctions are the primary class of conjunctions placed between words, phrases, clauses, and sentences that are of equal grammatical rank; the coordinating conjunctions are *for, and, nor, but, or, yet,* and *so*. A useful memorization trick is to remember that all the first letters of these conjunctions collectively spell the word fanboys.

> I need to go shopping, *but* I must be careful to leave enough money in the bank.
> She wore a black, red, *and* white shirt.

Subordinating conjunctions are the secondary class of conjunctions. They connect two unequal parts, one main (or independent) and the other subordinate (or dependent).

> I must go to the store *even though* I do not have enough money in the bank.

> *Because* I read the review, I do not want to go to the movie.

Notice that the presence of subordinating conjunctions makes clauses dependent. *I read the review* is an independent clause, but *because* makes the clause dependent. Thus, it needs an independent clause to complete the sentence.

Sentence Boundaries

Run-ons

A run-on is a sentence with too many independent clauses that are improperly connected to each other:

> This winter has been very cold some farmers have suffered damage to their crops.

The sentence above has two subject-verb combinations. The first is "this winter has been"; the second is "some farmers have suffered." However, they are simply stuck next to each other without any punctuation or conjunction. Therefore, the sentence is a run-on.

Another type of run-on occurs when writers use inappropriate punctuation:

> This winter has been very cold, some farmers have suffered damage to their crops.

Though a comma has been added, this sentence is still not correct. When a comma alone is used to join two independent clauses, it is known as a comma splice. Without an appropriate conjunction, a comma cannot join two independent clauses by itself.

Run-on sentences can be corrected by either dividing the independent clauses into two or more separate sentences or inserting appropriate conjunctions and/or punctuation. The run-on sentence can be amended by separating each subject-verb pair into its own sentence:

> This winter has been very cold. Some farmers have suffered damage to their crops.

The run-on can also be fixed by adding a comma and conjunction to join the two independent clauses with each other:

> This winter has been very cold, so some farmers have suffered damage to their crops.

Sentence Fragments

A complete sentence requires a verb and a subject that expresses a complete thought. Sometimes, the subject is omitted in the case of the implied *you*, used in sentences that are the command or imperative form—e.g., "Look!" or "Give me that." It is understood that the subject of the command is *you*, the listener or reader, so it is possible to have a structure without an explicit subject. Without these elements, though, the sentence is incomplete—it is a sentence fragment. While sentence fragments often occur in conversational English or creative writing, they are generally not appropriate in academic writing. Sentence fragments often occur when dependent clauses are not joined to an independent clause:

> *Sentence fragment*: Because the airline overbooked the flight.

The sentence above is a dependent clause that does not express a complete thought. What happened as a result of this cause? With the addition of an independent clause, this now becomes a complete sentence:

> *Complete sentence*: Because the airline overbooked the flight, several passengers were unable to board.

Sentences fragments may also occur through improper use of conjunctions:

> I'm going to the Bahamas for spring break. And to New York City for New Year's Eve.
>
> While the first sentence above is a complete sentence, the second one is not because it is a prepositional phrase that lacks a subject [I] and a verb [am going]. Joining the two together with the coordinating conjunction forms one grammatically-correct sentence:
>
> I'm going to the Bahamas for spring break and to New York City for New Year's Eve.

Recognition of Correct Sentences

Independent and Dependent Clauses

Independent and dependent clauses are strings of words that contain both a subject and a verb. An independent clause *can* stand alone as complete thought, but a dependent clause *cannot*. A dependent clause relies on other words to be a complete sentence.

> Independent clause: The keys are on the counter.
> Dependent clause: If the keys are on the counter

Notice that both clauses have a subject (*keys*) and a verb (*are*). The independent clause expresses a complete thought, but the word *if* at the beginning of the dependent clause makes it *dependent* on other words to be a complete thought.

> Independent clause: If the keys are on the counter, please give them to me.

This example constitutes a complete sentence since it includes at least one verb and one subject and is a complete thought. In this case, the independent clause has two subjects (*keys* & an implied *you*) and two verbs (*are* & *give*).

> Independent clause: I went to the store.
> Dependent clause: Because we are out of milk,

Complete Sentence: Because we are out of milk, I went to the store.
Complete Sentence: I went to the store because we are out of milk.

A *phrase* is a group of words that does not contain both a subject and a verb.

Sentence Fluency

Learning and utilizing the mechanics of structure will encourage effective, professional results, and adding some creativity will elevate one's writing to a higher level.

First, let's review the basic elements of sentences.

A *sentence* is a set of words that make up a grammatical unit. The words must have certain elements and be spoken or written in a specific order to constitute a complete sentence that makes sense.

1. A sentence must have a *subject* (a noun or noun phrase). The subject tells whom or what the sentence is addressing (i.e. what it is about).

2. A sentence must have an *action* or *state of being* (*a verb*). To reiterate: A verb forms the main part of the predicate of a sentence. This means that it explains what the noun is doing.

3. A sentence must convey a complete thought.

When examining writing, be mindful of grammar, structure, spelling, and patterns. Sentences can come in varying sizes and shapes; so, the point of grammatical correctness is not stamp out creativity or diversity in writing. Rather, grammatical correctness ensures that writing will be enjoyable and clear. One of the most common methods for catching errors is to mouth the words as you read them. Many typos are fixed automatically by our brain, but mouthing the words often circumvents this instinct and helps one read what's actually on the page. Often, grammar errors are caught not by memorization of grammar rules but by the training of one's mind to know whether something *sounds* right or not.

Types of Sentences

There isn't an overabundance of absolutes in grammar, but here is one: every sentence in the English language falls into one of four categories.

- Declarative: a simple statement that ends with a period

  The price of milk per gallon is the same as the price of gasoline.

- Imperative: a command, instruction, or request that ends with a period

  Buy milk when you stop to fill up your car with gas.

- Interrogative: a question that ends with a question mark

  Will you buy the milk?

- Exclamatory: a statement or command that expresses emotions like anger, urgency, or surprise and ends with an exclamation mark

  Buy the milk now!

Declarative sentences are the most common type, probably because they are comprised of the most general content, without any of the bells and whistles that the other three types contain. They are, simply, declarations or statements of any degree of seriousness, importance, or information.

Imperative sentences often seem to be missing a subject. The subject is there, though; it is just not visible or audible because it is *implied*. Look at the imperative example sentence.

Buy the milk when you fill up your car with gas.

You is the implied subject, the one to whom the command is issued. This is sometimes called *the understood you* because it is understood that *you* is the subject of the sentence.

Interrogative sentences—those that ask questions—are defined as such from the idea of the word *interrogation*, the action of questions being asked of suspects by investigators. Although that is serious business, interrogative sentences apply to all kinds of questions.

To exclaim is at the root of *exclamatory* sentences. These are made with strong emotions behind them. The only technical difference between a declarative or imperative sentence and an exclamatory one is the exclamation mark at the end. The example declarative and imperative sentences can both become an exclamatory one simply by putting an exclamation mark at the end of the sentences.

The price of milk per gallon is the same as the price of gasoline!
Buy milk when you stop to fill up your car with gas!

After all, someone might be really excited by the price of gas or milk, or they could be mad at the person that will be buying the milk! However, as stated before, exclamation marks in abundance defeat their own purpose! After a while, they begin to cause fatigue! When used only for their intended purpose, they can have their expected and desired effect.

Lengths

The ideal sentence length—the number of words in a sentence—depends upon the sentence's purpose.

It's okay for a sentence to be brief, and it's fine for a sentence to be lengthy. It's just important to make sure that long sentences do not become run-on sentences or too long to keep up with.

To keep writing interesting, vary sentence lengths, using a mixture of short, medium and long sentences.

Concord/Agreement

Antecedents

An *antecedent* is the noun to which a pronoun refers; it needs to be written or spoken before the pronoun is used. For many pronouns, antecedents are imperative for clarity. In particular, a lot of the personal, possessive, and demonstrative pronouns need antecedents. Otherwise, it would be unclear who or what someone is referring to when they use a pronoun like *he* or *this*.

Pronoun reference means that the pronoun should refer clearly to one, clear, unmistakable noun (the antecedent).

Pronoun-antecedent agreement refers to the need for the antecedent and the corresponding pronoun to agree in gender, person, and number. Here are some examples:

The *kidneys* (plural antecedent) are part of the urinary system. *They* (plural pronoun) serve several roles."

The kidneys are part of the *urinary system* (singular antecedent). *It* (singular pronoun) is also known as the renal system.

Pronoun Cases

The subjective pronouns —*I, you, he/she/it, we, they,* and *who*—are the subjects of the sentence.

Example: *They* have a new house.

The objective pronouns—*me, you (singular), him/her, us, them,* and *whom*—are used when something is being done for or given to someone; they are objects of the action.

Example: The teacher has an apple for *us*.

The possessive pronouns—*mine, my, your, yours, his, hers, its, their, theirs, our,* and *ours*—are used to denote that something (or someone) belongs to someone (or something).

Example: It's *their* chocolate cake.
Even Better Example: It's *my* chocolate cake!

One of the greatest challenges and worst abuses of pronouns concerns *who* and *whom*. Just knowing the following rule can eliminate confusion. *Who* is a subjective-case pronoun used only as a subject or subject complement. *Whom* is only objective-case and, therefore, the object of the verb or preposition.

Who is going to the concert?

You are going to the concert with *whom*?

Hint: When using *who* or *whom*, think of whether someone would say *he* or *him*. If the answer is *he*, use *who*. If the answer is *him*, use *whom*. This trick is easy to remember because *he* and *who* both end in vowels, and *him* and *whom* both end in the letter *M*.

Subject-Verb Agreement

The subject of a sentence and its verb must agree. The cornerstone rule of subject-verb agreement is that subject and verb must agree in number. Whether the subject is singular or plural, the verb must follow suit.

Incorrect: The houses is new.
Correct: The houses are new.
Also Correct: The house is new.

In other words, a singular subject requires a singular verb; a plural subject requires a plural verb. The words or phrases that come between the subject and verb do not alter this rule.

Incorrect: The houses built of brick is new.
Correct: The houses built of brick are new.

Incorrect: The houses with the sturdy porches is new.
Correct: The houses with the sturdy porches are new.

The subject will always follow the verb when a sentence begins with *here* or *there.* Identify these with care.

> Incorrect: Here *is* the *houses* with sturdy porches.
> Correct: Here *are* the *houses* with sturdy porches.

The subject in the sentences above is not *here*, it is *houses*. Remember, *here* and *there* are never subjects. Be careful that contractions such as *here's* or *there're* do not cause confusion!

Two subjects joined by *and* require a plural verb form, except when the two combine to make one thing:

> Incorrect: Garrett and Jonathan is over there.
> Correct: Garrett and Jonathan are over there.

> Incorrect: Spaghetti and meatballs are a delicious meal!
> Correct: Spaghetti and meatballs is a delicious meal!

In the example above, *spaghetti and meatballs* is a compound noun. However, *Garrett and Jonathan* is not a compound noun.

Two singular subjects joined by *or, either/or,* or *neither/nor* call for a singular verb form.

> Incorrect: Butter or syrup are acceptable.
> Correct: Butter or syrup is acceptable.

Plural subjects joined by *or*, *either/or*, or *neither/nor* are, indeed, plural.

> The chairs or the boxes are being moved next.

If one subject is singular and the other is plural, the verb should agree with the closest noun.

> Correct: The chair or the boxes are being moved next.
> Correct: The chairs or the box is being moved next.

Some plurals of money, distance, and time call for a singular verb.

> Incorrect: Three dollars *are* enough to buy that.
> Correct: Three dollars *is* enough to buy that.

For words declaring degrees of quantity such as *many of, some of,* or *most of,* let the noun that follows of be the guide:

> Incorrect: Many of the books is in the shelf.
> Correct: Many of the books are in the shelf.

> Incorrect: Most of the pie *are* on the table.
> Correct: Most of the pie *is* on the table.

For indefinite pronouns like anybody or everybody, use singular verbs.

> Everybody *is* going to the store.

However, the pronouns *few, many, several, all, some,* and *both* have their own rules and use plural forms.

Some *are* ready.

Some nouns like *crowd* and *congress* are called *collective nouns* and they require a singular verb form.

Congress *is* in session.
The news *is* over.

Books and movie titles, though, including plural nouns such as *Great Expectations*, also require a singular verb. Remember that only the subject affects the verb. While writing tricky subject-verb arrangements, say them aloud. Listen to them. Once the rules have been learned, one's ear will become sensitive to them, making it easier to pick out what's right and what's wrong.

Verbs

A verb is the part of speech that describes an action, state of being, or occurrence.

A *verb* forms the main part of a predicate of a sentence. This means that the verb explains what the noun (which will be discussed shortly) is doing. A simple example is *time flies*. The verb *flies* explains what the action of the noun, *time*, is doing. This example is a *main* verb.

Helping (*auxiliary*) verbs are words like *have, do, be, can, may, should, must,* and *will.* "I *should* go to the store." Helping verbs assist main verbs in expressing tense, ability, possibility, permission, or obligation.

Particles are minor function words like *not, in, out, up,* or *down* that become part of the verb itself. "I might *not*."

Participles are words formed from verbs that are often used to modify a noun, noun phrase, verb, or verb phrase.

The *running* teenager collided with the cyclist.

Participles can also create compound verb forms.

He is *speaking*.

Verbs have five basic forms: the *base* form, the *-s* form, the *-ing* form, the *past* form, and the *past participle* form.

The *past* forms are either *regular* (*love/loved; hate/hated*) or *irregular* because they don't end by adding the common past tense suffix "-ed" (*go/went; fall/fell; set/set*).

Verb Tense

Shifting verb forms entails conjugation, which is used to indicate tense, voice, or mood.

Verb tense is used to show when the action in the sentence took place. There are several different verb tenses, and it is important to know how and when to use them. Some verb tenses can be achieved by changing the form of the verb, while others require the use of helping verbs (e.g., *is, was,* or *has*).

- *Present tense* shows the action is happening currently or is ongoing:

  I walk to work every morning.

  She is stressed about the deadline.

- *Past tense* shows that the action happened in the past or that the state of being is in the past:

  I walked to work yesterday morning.

  She was stressed about the deadline.

- *Future tense* shows that the action will happen in the future or is a future state of being:

  I will walk to work tomorrow morning.

  She will be stressed about the deadline.

- *Present perfect tense* shows action that began in the past, but continues into the present:

  I have walked to work all week.

  She has been stressed about the deadline.

- *Past perfect tense* shows an action was finished before another took place:

  I had walked all week until I sprained my ankle.

  She had been stressed about the deadline until we talked about it.

- *Future perfect tense* shows an action that will be completed at some point in the future:

  By the time the bus arrives, I will have walked to work already.

Diction

An author's choice of words—also referred to as *diction*—helps to convey his or her meaning in a particular way. Through diction, an author can convey a particular tone—e.g., a humorous tone, a serious tone—in order to support the thesis in a meaningful way to the reader.

Identifying Variation in Dialect and Diction

Language arts educators often seem to be in the position of teaching the "right" way to use English, particularly in lessons about grammar and vocabulary. However, all it takes is back-to-back viewings of speeches by the queen of England and the president of the United States or side-by-side readings of a contemporary poem and one written in the 1600s to come to the conclusion that there is no single, fixed, correct form of spoken or written English. Instead, language varies and evolves across different regions and time periods. It also varies between cultural groups depending on factors such as race, ethnicity, age, and socioeconomic status. Students should come away from a language arts class with more than a strictly prescriptive view of language; they should have an appreciation for its rich diversity.

It is important to understand some key terms in discussing linguistic variety.

Language is a tool for communication. It may be spoken, unspoken—as with body language—written, or codified in other ways. Language is symbolic in the sense that it can describe objects, ideas, and events that are not actually present, have not actually occurred, or only exist in the mind of the speaker. All languages are governed by systematic rules of grammar and semantics. These rules allow speakers to manipulate a finite number of elements, such as sounds or written symbols, to create an infinite number of meanings.

A *dialect* is a distinct variety of a language in terms of patterns of grammar, vocabulary, and/or *phonology*—the sounds used by its speakers—that distinguish it from other forms of that language. Two dialects are not considered separate languages if they are *mutually intelligible*—if speakers of each dialect are able to understand one another. A dialect is not a subordinate version of a language. Examples of English dialects include Scottish English and American Southern English.

By definition, *Standard English* is a dialect. It is one variety of English with its own usage of grammar, vocabulary, and pronunciation. Given that Standard English is taught in schools and used in places like government, journalism, and other professional workplaces, it is often elevated above other English dialects. Linguistically, though, there is nothing that makes Standard English more correct or advanced than other dialects.

A *pidgin* is formed when speakers of different languages begin utilizing a simplified mixture of elements from both languages to communicate with each other. In North America, pidgins occurred when Africans were brought to European colonies as slaves, leading to a mixture of African and European languages. Historically, pidgins also sprung up in areas of international trade. A pidgin is communication born of necessity and lacks the full complexity or standardized rules that govern a language.

When a pidgin becomes widely used and is taught to children as their native language, it becomes a *Creole*. An example is Haitian Creole, a language based on French and including elements of West African languages.

An *accent* is a unique speech pattern, particularly in terms of tone or intonation. Speakers from different regions tend to have different accents, as do learners of English from different native languages. In some cases, accents are mutually intelligible, but in other cases, speakers with different accents might have some difficulty in understanding one another.

Colloquial language is language that is used conversationally or familiarly—e.g., "What's up?"—in contrast to formal, professional, or academic language—"How are you this evening?"

Vernacular refers to the native, everyday language of a place. Historically, for instance, Bibles and religious services across Europe were primarily offered in Latin, even centuries after the fall of the Roman Empire. After the revolution of the printing press and the widespread availability of vernacular translations of the Bible in the fifteenth and sixteenth centuries, everyday citizens were able to study from Bibles in their own language without needing specialized training in Latin.

A *regionalism* is a word or expression used in a particular region. In the United States, for instance, examples of regionalisms might be *soda*, *pop*, or *Coke*—terms that vary in popularity according to region.

Jargon is vocabulary used within a specialized field, such as computer programming or mechanics. Jargon may consist of specialized words or of everyday words that have a different meaning in this specialized context.

Slang refers to non-standard expressions that are not used in elevated speech and writing. Slang creates linguistic in-groups and out-groups of people, those who can understand the slang terms and those who can't. Slang is often tied to a specific time period. For example, "groovy" and "far out" are connected to the 1970s, and "as if!" and "4-1-1-" are connected to the 1990s.

Understanding Dialect and its Appropriateness

Certain forms of language are viewed differently depending on the context. Lessons learned in the classroom have a real-life application to a student's future, so he or she should know where, when, and how to utilize different forms of language.

Awareness of dialect can help students as readers. Many writers of literary fiction and nonfiction utilize dialect and colloquialisms to add verisimilitude to their writing. This is especially true for authors who focus on a particular region or cultural group in their works, also known as *regionalism* or *local color literature*. Examples include Zora Neale Hurston's *Their Eyes Were Watching God* and the short stories of Kate Chopin. Students can be asked to consider how the speech patterns in a text affect a reader's understanding of the characters—how the pattern reflects a character's background and place in society. They might consider a reader's impression of the region—how similar or different it is from the reader's region or what can be inferred about the region based on how people speak. In some cases, unfamiliar dialect may be very difficult for readers to understand on the page but becomes much more intelligible when read aloud—as in the reading of Shakespeare.

Connotation and Denotation

Connotation refers to the implied meaning of a word or phrase. Connotations are the ideas or feelings that words or phrases invoke other than their literal meaning. An example of the use of connotation is in people's use of the word *cheap*. While the literal meaning is something of low cost, people use the word to suggest something is poor in value or to negatively describe a person as reluctant to spend money. When something or someone is described this way, the reader is more inclined to have a particular image or feeling about it or him/her. Thus, connotation can be a very effective language tool in creating emotion and swaying opinion. However, connotations are sometimes hard to pin down because varying emotions can be associated with a word. Generally, though, connotative meanings tend to be fairly consistent within a specific cultural group.

Denotation is the literal definition of a word or phrase. The denotative meaning of a word is the one you would find in a dictionary. To present hard facts or vocabulary terms, it is helpful for a writer to use words which are mainly known for their denotative meanings rather than their connotative ones. In those instances, the words *inexpensive* and *frugal* are better because they do not carry the negative connotations that cheap does. *Inexpensive* refers to the cost of something, not its value, and *frugal* indicates that a person is conscientiously watching his or her spending. These terms do not elicit the same emotions that *cheap* does.

Authors sometimes choose to use both, but what they choose and when they use it is what critical readers need to differentiate. One method isn't inherently better than the other; however, one may create a better effect, depending upon an author's intent. If, for example, an author's purpose is to inform, to instruct, and to familiarize readers with a difficult subject, his or her use of connotation may be helpful. However, it may also undermine credibility and confuse readers. An author who wants to create a credible, scholarly effect in his or her text would most likely use denotation, which emphasizes literal, factual meaning and examples.

Technical Language

Test takers and critical readers alike should be very aware of technical language used within informational text. *Technical language* refers to terminology that is specific to a particular industry and is best understood by those specializing in that industry. This language is fairly easy to differentiate, since it will most likely be unfamiliar to readers. It's critical to be able to define technical language either by the author's written definition, through the use of an included glossary—if offered—or through context clues that help readers clarify word meaning.

Modifiers

Modifiers enhance meaning by clarifying or giving greater detail about another part of a sentence. However, incorrectly placed modifiers have the opposite effect and can cause confusion. A *misplaced modifier* is a modifier that is not located appropriately in relation to the word or phrase that it modifies:

> Because he was one of the greatest thinkers of Renaissance Italy, John idolized Leonardo da Vinci.

In this sentence, the modifier is "because he was one of the greatest thinkers of Renaissance Italy," and the noun it is intended to modify is "Leonardo da Vinci." However, due to the placement of the modifier next to the subject, John, it seems as if the sentence is stating that John was a Renaissance genius, not Da Vinci.

> John idolized Leonard da Vinci because he was one of the greatest thinkers of Renaissance Italy.

The modifier is now adjacent to the appropriate noun, clarifying which of the two men in this sentence is the greatest thinker.

Dangling modifiers modify a word or phrase that is not readily apparent in the sentence. That is, they "dangle" because they are not clearly attached to anything:

> After getting accepted to college, Amir's parents were proud.

The modifier here, "after getting accepted to college," should modify who got accepted. The noun immediately following the modifier is "Amir's parents"—but they are probably not the ones who are going to college.

> After getting accepted to college, Amir made his parents proud.

The subject of the sentence has been changed to Amir himself, and now the subject and its modifier are appropriately matched.

Idiom

A figure of speech (sometimes called an idiom) is a rhetorical device. It's a phrase that is not intended to be taken literally.

When the writer uses a figure of speech, their intention must be clear if it's to be used effectively. Some phrases can be interpreted in a number of ways, causing confusion for the reader. Look for clues to the writer's true intention to determine the best replacement. Likewise, some figures of speech may seem out of place in a more formal piece of writing. To show this, here is an example:

Seat belts save more lives than any other automobile safety feature. Many studies show that airbags save lives as well, however not all cars have airbags. For instance, some older cars don't. In addition, air bags aren't entirely reliable. For example, studies show that in 15% of accidents, airbags don't deploy as designed, but on the other hand seat belt malfunctions happen once in a blue moon.

Most people know that "once in a blue moon" refers to something that rarely happens. However, because the rest of the paragraph is straightforward and direct, using this figurative phrase distracts the reader. In this example, the earlier version is much more effective.

Now it's important to take a moment and review the meaning of the word *literally*. This is because it's one of the most misunderstood and misused words in the English language. *Literally* means that something is exactly what it says it is, and there can be no interpretation or exaggeration. Unfortunately, *literally* is often used for emphasis as in the following example:

> This morning, I literally couldn't get out of bed.

This sentence meant to say that the person was extremely tired and wasn't able to get up. However, the sentence can't *literally* be true unless that person was tied down to the bed, paralyzed, or affected by a strange situation that the writer (most likely) didn't intend. Here's another example:

> I literally died laughing.

The writer tried to say that something was very funny. However, unless they're writing this from beyond the grave, it can't *literally* be true.

Note that this doesn't mean that writers can't use figures of speech. The colorful use of language and idioms make writing more interesting and draw in the reader. However, for these kinds of expressions to be used correctly, they cannot include the word *literally*.

Active/Passive Voice

Active voice is a sentence structure in which the subject performs the action of the sentence. The verbs of these sentences are called *active verbs.*

> The deer jumped over the fence.

In the example above, the deer is the one jumping. *Passive voice* is a sentence structure in which the object performs the action of the sentence. The verbs of these sentences are called *passive verbs.*

> The fence was jumped by the deer.

In this example, the fence is the subject, but it is not jumping over anything. The deer is still the one performing the action, but it is now the object of the sentence.

Passive voice is helpful when it's unclear who performed an action.

The chair was moved.

While passive voice can add variety to writing, active voice is the generally preferred sentence structure.

Lack of Subject in Modifying Word Group

As stated above, a modifier is a word or phrase meant to describe or clarify another word in the sentence. When a sentence has a modifier but is missing the word it describes or clarifies, it's an error called a dangling modifier. We can fix the sentence by revising to include the word that is being modified. Consider the following examples with the modifier italicized:

Having walked five miles, this bench will be the place to rest. (Incorrect; this version of the sentence implies that the bench walked the miles, not the person.)

Having walked five miles, Matt will rest on this bench. (Correct; in this version, *having walked five miles* correctly modifies *Matt*, who did the walking.)

Since midnight, my dreams have been pleasant and comforting. (Incorrect; in this version, the adverb clause *since midnight* cannot modify the noun *dreams.*)

Since midnight, I have had pleasant and comforting dreams. (Correct; in this version, *since midnight* modifies the verb *have had*, telling us when the dreams occurred.)

Sometimes the modifier is not located close enough to the word it modifies for the sentence to be clearly understood. In this case, we call the error a misplaced modifier. Here is an example with the modifier italicized and the modified word in underlined.

We gave the hot <u>cocoa</u> to the children *that was filled with marshmallows.* (Incorrect; this sentence implies that the children are what are filled with marshmallows.)

We gave the hot <u>*cocoa*</u> *that was filled with marshmallows* to the children. (Correct; here, the cocoa is filled with marshmallows. The modifier is near the word it modifies.)

Logical Comparison

Presenting Information Clearly, Concisely, and Logically

All information should be presented with a clear beginning, middle, and end. Distinct organization always makes any work more clear, concise, and logical. For a presentation, this should involve choosing a primary topic and then discussing it in the following format:

- Introducing the speaker and the main topic
- Providing evidence, supporting details, further explanation of the topic in the main body
- Concluding it with a firm resolution and repetition of the main point

The beginning, middle, and end should also be linked with effective transitions that make the presentation flow well. For example, a presentation should always begin with an introduction by the speaker, including what he/she does and what he/she is there to present. Good transitional introductions may begin with statements such as *For those who do not know me, my name is..., As many of you know, I am...* or *Good morning everyone, my name is ___, and I am the new project manager.* A good introduction grabs the attention and interest of the audience.

After an introduction has been made, the speaker will then want to state the purpose of the presentation with a natural transition, such as *I am here to discuss the latest editions to our standard of procedure...* or *This afternoon, I would like to present the results of our latest findings.* Once the purpose has been identified, the speaker will want to adhere to the main idea announced. The presenter should be certain to keep the main idea to one sentence as too much information can confuse an audience; an introduction should be succinct and to the point.

Supporting information should always be presented in concise, easy-to-read formats such as bullet points or lists—if visual aids are presented during the presentation. Good transitions such as *Let's begin with...* or *Now to look at...* make the presentation flow smoothly and logically, helping listeners to keep ideas organized as they are presented. Keeping the material concise is extremely important in a presentation, and visual aids should be used only to emphasize points or explain ideas. All the supporting information should relate back to the main idea, avoiding unnecessary tangents.

Finally, a firm conclusion involves repeating the main point of the presentation by either inspiring listeners to act or by reiterating the most important points made in the speech. It should also include an expression of gratitude to the audience as well as transition to opening the floor for questions.

Logical Agreement

Agreement in Number

Subjects and verbs must agree in number. If a sentence has a singular subject, then it must use a singular verb. If there is a plural subject, then it must use a plural verb.

Singular Noun	Singular Verb	Plural Noun	Plural verb
Man	has	men	have
child	plays	children	play
basketball	bounces	basketballs	bounce

Agreement in Person

Verbs must also agree in person. A subject that uses first person must include a verb that is also in first person. The same is true for second and third person subjects and verbs.

	Noun	Verb
First person	I	am
Second person	you	are
Third person	she	is

Common Agreement Errors

Compound Subjects

Compound subjects are when two or more subjects are joined by a coordinating conjunction, such as *and, or, neither,* or *nor*. Errors in agreement sometimes occur when there is a compound subject:

Incorrect: Mike and I am in a meeting this morning.

Correct: Mike and I are in a meeting this morning.

A compound subject always uses the plural form of the verb to match with the plural subject. In the above example, readers can substitute "Mike and I" for "we" to make it easier to determine the verb: "We *are* in a meeting this morning."

Separation of Subject and Verb

Errors sometimes occur when the subject is separated from the verb by a prepositional phrase or parenthetical element:

Incorrect: The objective of the teachers are to help students learn.

Correct: The objective of the teachers is to help students learn.

The verb must agree with the singular subject *objective*, not the word *teachers*, which is the object of the preposition *of* and does not influence the subject. An easy way to determine if the subject and verb agree is to take out the middle preposition: "The objective *is* to help students learn."

Indefinite Pronouns

Indefinite pronouns refer to people or groups in a general way: *each, anyone, none, all, either, neither,* and *everyone.* Some indefinite pronouns are always singular, such as *each, everyone, someone*, and *everybody*, which affects verb choice:

Incorrect: Each of them are competing in the race.

Correct: Each of them is competing in the race.

While the word *them* can indicate that a plural verb is needed, the subject *each* is singular regardless of what it refers to, requiring the singular verb, *is*.

Other indefinite pronouns can be singular or plural, depending on what they are referring to, such as *anyone, all,* and *some.*

Some of the orders are scheduled to arrive today.

Some refers to *orders*, which is plural, so the plural verb (*are*) is needed.

Some of the cake is left on the dining room table.

Some refers to *cake*, which is singular, so the singular verb (*is*) is needed.

Subjects Joined by Or and Nor

Compound subjects joined by *or* or *nor* rely on the subject nearest to the verb to determine conjugation and agreement:

Neither Ben nor Jeff was in attendance at the conference.

Pink or purple is the bride's color choice.

In each example, the subjects are both singular, so the verb should be singular.

If one subject is singular and the other plural, the subject nearest to the verb is the one that needs to agree:

Either the shirt or pants are hanging on the clothesline.

In this example there is a singular subject (*shirt*) and a plural subject (*pants*), so the verb (*are*) should agree with the subject nearest to it (*pants*).

Punctuation

Capitalization

Here's a non-exhaustive list of things that should be capitalized.

- The first word of every sentence
- The first word of every line of poetry
- The first letter of proper nouns (World War II)
- Holidays (Valentine's Day)
- The days of the week and months of the year (Tuesday, March)
- The first word, last word, and all major words in the titles of books, movies, songs, and other creative works (In the novel, *To Kill a Mockingbird*, note that *a* is lowercase since it's not a major word, but *to* is capitalized since it's the first word of the title.)
- Titles when preceding a proper noun (President Roberto Gonzales, Aunt Judy)

When simply using a word such as president or secretary, though, the word is not capitalized.

Officers of the new business must include a *president* and *treasurer*.

Seasons—spring, fall, etc.—are not capitalized.

North, *south*, *east*, and *west* are capitalized when referring to regions but are not when being used for directions. In general, if it's preceded by *the* it should be capitalized.

I'm from the South.
I drove south.

Ellipses

An *ellipsis* (. . .) consists of three handy little dots that can speak volumes on behalf of irrelevant material. Writers use them in place of words, lines, phrases, list content, or paragraphs that might just as easily have been omitted from a passage of writing. This can be done to save space or to focus only on the specifically relevant material.

Exercise is good for some unexpected reasons. Watkins writes, "Exercise has many benefits such as . . . reducing cancer risk."

In the example above, the ellipsis takes the place of the other benefits of exercise that are more expected.

The ellipsis may also be used to show a pause in sentence flow.

"I'm wondering . . . how this could happen," Dylan said in a soft voice.

Commas

A *comma* (,) is the punctuation mark that signifies a pause—breath—between parts of a sentence. It denotes a break of flow. As with so many aspects of writing structure, authors will benefit by reading their writing aloud or mouthing the words. This can be particularly helpful if one is uncertain about whether the comma is needed.

In a complex sentence—one that contains a subordinate (dependent) clause or clauses—the use of a comma is dictated by where the subordinate clause is located. If the subordinate clause is located before the main clause, a comma is needed between the two clauses.

I will not pay for the steak, *because I don't have that much money.*

Generally, if the subordinate clause is placed after the main clause, no punctuation is needed.

I did well on my exam because I studied two hours the night before.

Notice how the last clause is dependent, because it requires the earlier independent clauses to make sense.

Use a comma on both sides of an interrupting phrase.

I will pay for the ice cream, *chocolate and vanilla*, and then will eat it all myself.

The words forming the phrase in italics are nonessential (extra) information. To determine if a phrase is nonessential, try reading the sentence without the phrase and see if it's still coherent.

A comma is not necessary in this next sentence because no interruption—nonessential or extra information—has occurred. Read sentences aloud when uncertain.

I will pay for his chocolate and vanilla ice cream and then will eat it all myself.

If the nonessential phrase comes at the beginning of a sentence, a comma should only go at the end of the phrase. If the phrase comes at the end of a sentence, a comma should only go at the beginning of the phrase.

Other types of interruptions include the following:

- interjections: Oh no, I am not going.
- abbreviations: Barry Potter, M.D., specializes in heart disorders.
- direct addresses: Yes, Claudia, I am tired and going to bed.
- parenthetical phrases: His wife, lovely as she was, was not helpful.
- transitional phrases: Also, it is not possible.

The second comma in the following sentence is called an Oxford comma.

I will pay for ice cream, syrup, and pop.

It is a comma used after the second-to-last item in a series of three or more items. It comes before the word *or* or *and*. Not everyone uses the Oxford comma; it is optional, but many believe it is needed. The comma functions as a tool to reduce confusion in writing. So, if omitting the Oxford comma would cause confusion, then it's best to include it.

Commas are used in math to mark the place of thousands in numerals, breaking them up so they are easier to read. Other uses for commas are in dates (*March 19, 2016*), letter greetings (*Dear Sally,*), and in between cities and states (*Louisville, KY*).

Semicolons

The *semicolon* (;) might be described as a heavy-handed comma. Take a look at these two examples:

I will pay for the ice cream, but I will not pay for the steak.
I will pay for the ice cream; I will not pay for the steak.

What's the difference? The first example has a comma and a conjunction separating the two independent clauses. The second example does not have a conjunction, but there are two independent clauses in the sentence. So something more than a comma is required. In this case, a semicolon is used.

Two independent clauses can only be joined in a sentence by either a comma and conjunction or a semicolon. If one of those tools is not used, the sentence will be a run-on. Remember that while the clauses are independent, they need to be closely related in order to be contained in one sentence.

Another use for the semicolon is to separate items in a list when the items themselves require commas.

The family lived in Phoenix, Arizona; Oklahoma City, Oklahoma; and Raleigh, North Carolina.

Colons

Colons have many miscellaneous functions. Colons can be used to precede further information or a list. In these cases, a colon should only follow an independent clause.

Humans take in sensory information through five basic senses: sight, hearing, smell, touch, and taste.

The meal includes the following components:

- Caesar salad
- spaghetti
- garlic bread
- cake

The family got what they needed: a reliable vehicle.

While a comma is more common, a colon can also precede a formal quotation.

He said to the crowd: "Let's begin!"

The colon is used after the greeting in a formal letter.

Dear Sir:
To Whom It May Concern:

In the writing of time, the colon separates the minutes from the hour (*4:45 p.m.*). The colon can also be used to indicate a ratio between two numbers (*50:1*).

Hyphens

The *hyphen* (-) is a little hash mark that can be used to join words to show that they are linked.

Hyphenate two words that work together as a single adjective (a compound adjective).

honey-covered biscuits

Some words always require hyphens, even if not serving as an adjective.

merry-go-round

Hyphens always go after certain prefixes like *anti-* & *all-*.

Hyphens should also be used when the absence of the hyphen would cause a strange vowel combination (*semi-engineer*) or confusion. For example, *re-collect* should be used to describe something being gathered twice rather than being written as *recollect*, which means to remember.

Parentheses and Dashes

Parentheses are half-round brackets that look like this: ( ). They set off a word, phrase, or sentence that is an afterthought, explanation, or side note relevant to the surrounding text but not essential. A pair of commas is often used to set off this sort of information, but parentheses are generally used for information that would not fit well within a sentence or that the writer deems not important enough to be structurally part of the sentence.

The picture of the heart (see above) shows the major parts you should memorize.
Mount Everest is one of three mountains in the world that are over 28,000 feet high (K2 and Kanchenjunga are the other two).

See how the sentences above are complete without the parenthetical statements? In the first example, *see above* would not have fit well within the flow of the sentence. The second parenthetical statement could have been a separate sentence, but the writer deemed the information not pertinent to the topic.

The **em-dash** (—) is a mark longer than a hyphen used as a punctuation mark in sentences and to set apart a relevant thought. Even after plucking out the line separated by the dash marks, the sentence will be intact and make sense.

Looking out the airplane window at the landmarks—Lake Clarke, Thompson Community College, and the bridge—she couldn't help but feel excited to be home.

The dashes use is similar to that of parentheses or a pair of commas. So, what's the difference? Many believe that using dashes makes the clause within them stand out while using parentheses is subtler. It's advised to not use dashes when commas could be used instead.

Quotation Marks

Here are some instances where *quotation marks* should be used:

- Dialogue for characters in narratives. When characters speak, the first word should always be capitalized, and the punctuation goes inside the quotes. For example:

  Janie said, "The tree fell on my car during the hurricane."

- Around titles of songs, short stories, essays, and chapter in books
- To emphasize a certain word
- To refer to a word as the word itself

Apostrophes

This punctuation mark, the apostrophe ('), is a versatile little mark. It has a few different functions:

- Quotes: Apostrophes are used when a second quote is needed within a quote.

  In my letter to my friend, I wrote, "The girl had to get a new purse, and guess what Mary did? She said, 'I'd like to go with you to the store.' I knew Mary would buy it for her."

- Contractions: Another use for an apostrophe in the quote above is a contraction. *I'd* is used for *I would.*

- Possession: An apostrophe followed by the letter *s* shows possession (*Mary's* purse). If the possessive word is plural, the apostrophe generally just follows the word.

  The trees' leaves are all over the ground.

Practice Questions

1. Which of the following sentences uses correct punctuation?
   a. Carole is not currently working; her focus is on her children at the moment.
   b. Carole is not currently working and her focus is on her children at the moment.
   c. Carole is not currently working, her focus is on her children at the moment.
   d. Carole is not currently working her focus is on her children at the moment.

2. Which of these examples shows incorrect use of subject-verb agreement?
   a. Neither of the cars are parked on the street.
   b. Both of my kids are going to camp this summer.
   c. Any of your friends are welcome to join us on the trip in November.
   d. Each of the clothing options is appropriate for the job interview.

3. Which of the following passages best displays clarity, fluency, and parallelism?
   a. Ernest Hemingway is probably the most noteworthy of expatriate authors. Hemingway's concise writing style, void of emotion and stream of consciousness, had a lasting impact, one which resonates to this very day. In Hemingway's novels, much like in American cinema, the hero acts without thinking, is living in the moment, and is repressing physical and emotional pain.
   b. Ernest Hemingway is probably the most noteworthy of expatriate authors since his concise writing style is void of emotion and stream of consciousness and has had a lasting impact on Americans which has resonated to this very day, and Hemingway's novels are much like in American cinema. The hero acts. He doesn't think. He lives in the moment. He represses physical and emotional pain.
   c. Ernest Hemingway is probably the most noteworthy of authors. His concise writing style, void of emotion and consciousness, had a lasting impact, one which resonates to this very day. In Hemingway's novels, much like in American cinema, the hero acts without thinking, lives in the moment, and represses physical and emotional pain.
   d. Ernest Hemingway is probably the most noteworthy of expatriate authors. His concise writing style, void of emotion and stream of consciousness, had a lasting impact, one which resonates to this very day. In Hemingway's novels, much like in American cinema, the hero acts without thinking, lives in the moment, and represses physical and emotional pain.

4. What is the noun phrase in the following sentence?

   Charlotte's new German shepherd puppy is energetic.

   a. Puppy
   b. Charlotte
   c. German shepherd puppy
   d. Charlotte's new German shepherd puppy

5. The following sentence contains what kind of error?

Forgetting that he was supposed to meet his girlfriend for dinner, Anita was mad when Fred showed up late.

a. Parallelism
b. Run-on sentence
c. Misplaced modifier
d. Subject-verb agreement

Answer Explanations

1. A: Choice *A* is correctly punctuated because it uses a semicolon to join two independent clauses that are related in meaning. Each of these clauses could function as an independent sentence. Choice *B* is incorrect because the conjunction is not preceded by a comma. A comma and conjunction should be used together to join independent clauses. Choice *C* is incorrect because a comma should only be used to join independent sentences when it also includes a coordinating conjunction such as *and* or *so*. Choice *D* does not use punctuation to join the independent clauses, so it is considered a fused (same as a run-on) sentence.

2. A: Choice *A* uses incorrect subject-verb agreement because the indefinite pronoun *neither* is singular and must use the singular verb form *is*. The pronoun *both* is plural and uses the plural verb form of *are*. The pronoun *any* can be either singular or plural. In this example, it is used as a plural, so the plural verb form *are* is used. The pronoun *each* is singular and uses the singular verb form *is*.

3. D: This passage displays clarity (the author states precisely what he or she intended), fluency (the sentences run smoothly together), and parallelism (words are used in a similar fashion to help provide rhythm). Choice *A* lacks parallelism. When the author states, "the hero acts without thinking, is living in the moment, and is repressing physical and emotional pain," the words *acts, is living* and *is repressing* are in different tenses, and, consequently, jarring to one's ears. Choice *B* runs on endlessly in the first half ("Ernest Hemingway is probably the most noteworthy of expatriate authors since his concise writing style is void of emotion and stream of consciousness and has had a lasting impact on Americans which has resonated to this very day, and Hemingway's novels are much like in American cinema.") It demands some type of pause and strains the readers' eyes. The second half of the passage is choppy: "The hero acts. He doesn't think. He lives in the moment. He represses physical and emotional pain." For Choice *C*, leaving out *expatriate* is, first, vague, and second, alters the meaning. The correct version claims that Hemingway was the most notable of the expatriate authors while the second version claims he's the most notable of any author *ever*, a very bold claim indeed. Also, leaving out *stream of* in "stream of consciousness" no longer references the non-sequential manner in which most people think. Instead, this version sounds like all the characters in the novel are in a coma!

4. D: A noun phrase consists of the noun and all of its modifiers. In this case, the subject of the sentence is the noun *puppy*, but it is preceded by several modifiers—adjectives that give more information about what kind of puppy, which are also part of the noun phrase. Thus, *A* is incorrect. Charlotte is the owner of the puppy and a modifier of the puppy, so *B* is false. *C* is incorrect because it contains some, but not all, of the modifiers pertaining to the puppy. *D* is correct because it contains all of them.

5. C: In this sentence, the modifier is the phrase "Forgetting that he was supposed to meet his girlfriend for dinner." This phrase offers information about Fred's actions, but the noun that immediately follows it is Anita, creating some confusion about the "do-er" of the phrase. A more appropriate sentence arrangement would be "Forgetting that he was supposed to meet his girlfriend for dinner, Fred made Anita mad when he showed up late." *A* is incorrect as parallelism refers to the consistent use of sentence structure and verb tense, and this sentence is appropriately consistent. *B* is incorrect as a run-on sentence does not contain appropriate punctuation for the number of independent clauses presented, which is not true of this description. *D* is incorrect because subject-verb agreement refers to the appropriate conjugation of a verb relative to the subject, and all verbs have been properly conjugated.

Revision Skills

Organization

Good writing is not merely a random collection of sentences. No matter how well written, sentences must relate and coordinate appropriately with one another. If not, the writing seems random, haphazard, and disorganized. Therefore, good writing must be organized, where each sentence fits a larger context and relates to the sentences around it.

Transition Words

The writer should act as a guide, showing the reader how all the sentences fit together. Consider the seat belt example again:

> Seat belts save more lives than any other automobile safety feature. Many studies show that airbags save lives as well. Not all cars have airbags. Many older cars don't. Air bags aren't entirely reliable. Studies show that in 15% of accidents, airbags don't deploy as designed. Seat belt malfunctions are extremely rare.

There's nothing wrong with any of these sentences individually, but together they're disjointed and difficult to follow. The best way for the writer to communicate information is through the use of transition words. Here are examples of transition words and phrases that tie sentences together, enabling a more natural flow:

- To show causality: *as a result*, *therefore*, and *consequently*
- To compare and contrast: *however*, *but*, and *on the other hand*
- To introduce examples: *for instance*, *namely*, and *including*
- To show order of importance: *foremost*, *primarily*, *secondly*, and *lastly*

NOTE: This is not a complete list of transitions. There are many more that can be used; however, most fit into these or similar categories. The important point is that the words should clearly show the relationship between sentences, supporting information, and the main idea.

Here is an update to the previous example using transition words. These changes make it easier to read and bring clarity to the writer's points:

> Seat belts save more lives than any other automobile safety feature. Many studies show that airbags save lives as well; however, not all cars have airbags. For instance, some older cars don't. Furthermore, air bags aren't entirely reliable. For example, studies show that in 15% of accidents, airbags don't deploy as designed, but, on the other hand, seat belt malfunctions are extremely rare.

Also, be prepared to analyze whether the writer is using the best transition word or phrase for the situation. Take this sentence for example: "As a result, seat belt malfunctions are extremely rare." This sentence doesn't make sense in the context above because the writer is trying to show the contrast between seat belts and airbags, not the causality.

Logical Sequence

Even if the writer includes plenty of information to support their point, the writing is only coherent when the information is in a logical order. First, the writer should introduce the main idea, whether for a paragraph, a section, or the entire piece. Second, they should present evidence to support the main idea by using transitional language. This shows the reader how the information relates to the main idea and to the sentences around it. The writer should then take time to interpret the information, making sure necessary connections are obvious to the reader. Finally, the writer can summarize the information in a closing section.

Though most writing follows this pattern, it isn't a set rule. Sometimes writers change the order for effect. For example, the writer can begin with a surprising piece of supporting information to grab the reader's attention, and then transition to the main idea. Thus, if a passage doesn't follow the logical order, don't immediately assume it's wrong. However, most writing usually settles into a logical sequence after a nontraditional beginning.

Introductions and Conclusions

Examining the writer's strategies for introductions and conclusions puts the reader in the right mindset to interpret the rest of the text. Look for methods the writer might use for introductions such as:

- Stating the main point immediately, followed by outlining how the rest of the piece supports this claim.
- Establishing important, smaller pieces of the main idea first, and then grouping these points into a case for the main idea.
- Opening with a quotation, anecdote, question, seeming paradox, or other piece of interesting information, and then using it to lead to the main point.

Whatever method the writer chooses, the introduction should make their intention clear, establish their voice as a credible one, and encourage a person to continue reading.

Conclusions tend to follow a similar pattern. In them, the writer restates their main idea a final time, often after summarizing the smaller pieces of that idea. If the introduction uses a quote or anecdote to grab the reader's attention, the conclusion often makes reference to it again. Whatever way the writer chooses to arrange the conclusion, the final restatement of the main idea should be clear and simple for the reader to interpret. Finally, conclusions shouldn't introduce any new information.

Evaluation of Evidence

Evaluating a Passage

Determining conclusions requires being an active reader, as a reader must make a prediction and analyze facts to identify a conclusion. There are a few ways to determine a logical conclusion, but careful reading is the most important. It's helpful to read a passage a few times, noting details that seem important to the piece. A reader should also identify key words in a passage to determine the logical conclusion or determination that flows from the information presented.

Textual evidence within the details helps readers draw a conclusion about a passage. *Textual evidence* refers to information—facts and examples that support the main point. Textual evidence will likely come from outside sources and can be in the form of quoted or paraphrased material. In order to draw a conclusion from evidence, it's important to examine the credibility and validity of that evidence as well as how (and if) it relates to the main idea.

If an author presents a differing opinion or a *counter-argument* in order to refute it, the reader should consider how and why this information is being presented. It is meant to strengthen the original argument and shouldn't be confused with the author's intended conclusion, but it should also be considered in the reader's final evaluation.

Sometimes, authors explicitly state the conclusion they want readers to understand. Alternatively, a conclusion may not be directly stated. In that case, readers must rely on the implications to form a logical conclusion:

> On the way to the bus stop, Michael realized his homework wasn't in his backpack. He ran back to the house to get it and made it back to the bus just in time.

In this example, though it's never explicitly stated, it can be inferred that Michael is a student on his way to school in the morning. When forming a conclusion from implied information, it's important to read the text carefully to find several pieces of evidence to support the conclusion.

Summarizing is an effective way to draw a conclusion from a passage. A summary is a shortened version of the original text, written by the reader in his/her own words. Focusing on the main points of the original text and including only the relevant details can help readers reach a conclusion. It's important to retain the original meaning of the passage.

Like summarizing, *paraphrasing* can also help a reader fully understand different parts of a text. Paraphrasing calls for the reader to take a small part of the passage and list or describe its main points. Paraphrasing is more than rewording the original passage, though. It should be written in the reader's own words, while still retaining the meaning of the original source. This will indicate an understanding of the original source, yet still help the reader expand on his/her interpretation.

Readers should pay attention to the *sequence*, or the order in which details are laid out in the text, as this can be important to understanding its meaning as a whole. Writers will often use transitional words to help the reader understand the order of events and to stay on track. Words like *next, then, after*, and *finally* show that the order of events is important to the author. In some cases, the author omits these transitional words, and the sequence is implied. Authors may even purposely present the information out of order to make an impact or have an effect on the reader. An example might be when a narrative writer uses *flashback* to reveal information.

Responding to a Passage

There are a few ways for readers to engage actively with the text, such as making inferences and predictions. An *inference* refers to a point that is implied (as opposed to directly-stated) by the evidence presented:

> Bradley packed up all of the items from his desk in a box and said goodbye to his coworkers for the last time.

From this sentence, though it is not directly stated, readers can infer that Bradley is leaving his job. It's necessary to use inference in order to draw conclusions about the meaning of a passage. Authors make implications through character dialogue, thoughts, effects on others, actions, and looks. Like in life, readers must assemble all the clues to form a complete picture.

When making an inference about a passage, it's important to rely only on the information that is provided in the text itself. This helps readers ensure that their conclusions are valid.

Readers will also find themselves making predictions when reading a passage or paragraph. *Predictions* are guesses about what's going to happen next. Readers can use prior knowledge to help make accurate predictions. Prior knowledge is best utilized when readers make links between the current text, previously read texts, and life experiences. Some texts use suspense and foreshadowing to captivate readers:

A cat darted across the street just as the car came careening around the curve.

One unfortunate prediction might be that the car will hit the cat. Of course, predictions aren't always accurate, so it's important to read carefully to the end of the text to determine the accuracy of predictions.

Awareness of Audience, Tone, and Purpose

Determining the Appropriate Mode of Writing

The author's *primary purpose* is defined as the reason an author chooses to write a selection, and it is often dependent on his or her *audience*. A biologist writing a textbook, for example, does so to communicate scientific knowledge to an audience of people who want to study biology. An audience can be as broad as the entire global population or as specific as women fighting for equal rights in the bicycle repair industry. Whatever the audience, it is important that the author considers its demographics—age, gender, culture, language, education level, etc.

If the author's purpose is to persuade or inform, he or she will consider how much the intended audience knows about the subject. For example, if an author is writing on the importance of recycling to anyone who will listen, he or she will use the informative mode—including background information on recycling—and the argumentative mode—evidence for why it works, while also using simple diction so that it is easy for everyone to understand. If, on the other hand, the writer is proposing new methods for recycling using solar energy, the audience is probably already familiar with standard recycling processes and will require less background information, as well as more technical language inherent to the scientific community.

If the author's purpose is to entertain through a story or a poem, he or she will need to consider whom he/she is trying to entertain. If an author is writing a script for a children's cartoon, the plot, language, conflict, characters, and humor would align with the interests of the age demographic of that audience. On the other hand, if an author is trying to entertain adults, he or she may write content not suitable for children. The author's purpose and audience are generally interdependent.

Identifying the Tone, Purpose, and Intended Audience

An author's *writing style*—the way in which words, grammar, punctuation, and sentence fluidity are used—is the most influential element in a piece of writing, and it is dependent on the purpose and the audience for whom it is intended. Together, a writing style and mode of writing form the foundation of a written work, and a good writer will choose the most effective mode and style to convey a message to readers.

Writers should first determine what they are trying to say and then choose the most effective mode of writing to communicate that message. Different writing modes and *word choices* will affect the tone of a piece—that is, its underlying attitude, emotion, or character. The argumentative mode may utilize words that are earnest, angry, passionate, or excited whereas an informative piece may have a sterile, germane, or enthusiastic tone. The tones found in narratives vary greatly, depending on the purpose of the writing. *Tone* will also be affected by the audience—teaching science to children or those who may be uninterested would be most effective with enthusiastic language and exclamation points whereas teaching science to college students may take on a more serious and professional tone, with fewer charged words and punctuation choices that are inherent to academia.

Sentence fluidity—whether sentences are long and rhythmic or short and succinct—also affects a piece of writing as it determines the way in which a piece is read. Children or audiences unfamiliar with a subject do better with short, succinct sentence structures as these break difficult concepts up into shorter points. A period, question mark, or exclamation point is literally a signal for the reader to stop and takes more time to process. Thus, longer, more complex sentences are more appropriate for adults or educated audiences as they can fit more information in between processing time.

The amount of *supporting detail* provided is also tailored to the audience. A text that introduces a new subject to its readers will focus more on broad ideas without going into greater detail whereas a text that focuses on a more specific subject is likely to provide greater detail about the ideas discussed.

Writing styles, like modes, are most effective when tailored to their audiences. Having awareness of an audience's demographic is one of the most crucial aspects of properly communicating an argument, a story, or a set of information.

Choosing the Most Appropriate Type of Writing

Before beginning any writing, it is imperative that a writer have a firm grasp on the message he or she wishes to convey and how he or she wants readers to be affected by the writing. For example, does the author want readers to be more informed about the subject? Does the writer want readers to agree with his or her opinion? Does the writer want readers to get caught up in an exciting narrative? The following steps are a guide to determining the appropriate type of writing for a task, purpose, and audience:

1. Identifying the purpose for writing the piece
2. Determining the audience
3. Adapting the writing mode, word choices, tone, and style to fit the audience and the purpose

It is important to distinguish between a work's purpose and its main idea. The essential difference between the two is that the *main idea* is what the author wants to communicate about the topic at hand whereas the *primary purpose* is why the author is writing in the first place. The primary purpose is what will determine the type of writing an author will choose to utilize, not the main idea, though the two are related. For example, if an author writes an article on the mistreatment of animals in factory farms and, at the end, suggests that people should convert to vegetarianism, the main idea is that vegetarianism would reduce the poor treatment of animals. The primary purpose is to convince the reader to stop eating animals. Since the primary purpose is to galvanize an audience into action, the author would choose the argumentative writing mode.

The next step is to consider to whom the author is appealing as this will determine the type of details to be included, the diction to be used, the tone to be employed, and the sentence structure to be used. An audience can be identified by considering the following questions:

- What is the purpose for writing the piece?
- To whom is it being written?
- What is their age range?

- Are they familiar with the material being presented, or are they just being newly introduced to it?
- Where are they from?
- Is the task at hand in a professional or casual setting?
- Is the task at hand for monetary gain?

These are just a few of the numerous considerations to keep in mind, but the main idea is to become as familiar with the audience as possible. Once the audience has been understood, the author can then adapt the writing style to align with the readers' education and interests. The audience is what determines the *rhetorical appeal* the author will use—ethos, pathos, or logos. *Ethos* is a rhetorical appeal to an audience's ethics and/or morals. Ethos is most often used in argumentative and informative writing modes. *Pathos* is an appeal to the audience's emotions and sympathies, and it is found in argumentative, descriptive, and narrative writing modes. *Logos* is an appeal to the audience's logic and reason and is used primarily in informative texts as well as in supporting details for argumentative pieces. Rhetorical appeals are discussed in depth in the informational texts and rhetoric section of the test.

If the author is trying to encourage global conversion to vegetarianism, he or she may choose to use all three rhetorical appeals to reach varying personality types. Those who are less interested in the welfare of animals but are interested in facts and science would relate more to logos. Animal lovers would relate better to an emotional appeal. In general, the most effective works utilize all three appeals.

Finally, after determining the writing mode and rhetorical appeal, the author will consider word choice, sentence structure, and tone, depending on the purpose and audience. The author may choose words that convey sadness or anger when speaking about animal welfare if writing to persuade, or he or she will stick to dispassionate and matter-of-fact tones, if informing the public on the treatment of animals in factory farms. If the author is writing to a younger or less-educated audience, he or she may choose to shorten and simplify sentence structures and word choice. If appealing to an audience with more expert knowledge on a particular subject, writers will more likely employ a style of longer sentences and more complex vocabulary.

Depending on the task, the author may choose to use a first person, second person, or third person point of view. First person and second person perspectives are inherently more casual in tone, including the author and the reader in the rhetoric, while third person perspectives are often seen in more professional settings.

Evaluating the Effectiveness of a Piece of Writing

An effective and engaging piece of writing will cause the reader to forget about the author entirely. Readers will become so engrossed in the subject, argument, or story at hand that they will almost identify with it, readily adopting beliefs proposed by the author or accepting all elements of the story as believable. On the contrary, poorly written works will cause the reader to be hyperaware of the author, doubting the writer's knowledge of a subject or questioning the validity of a narrative. Persuasive or expository works that are poorly researched will have this effect, as well as poorly planned stories with significant plot holes. An author must consider the task, purpose, and audience to sculpt a piece of writing effectively.

When evaluating the effectiveness of a piece, the most important thing to consider is how well the purpose is conveyed to the audience through the mode, use of rhetoric, and writing style.

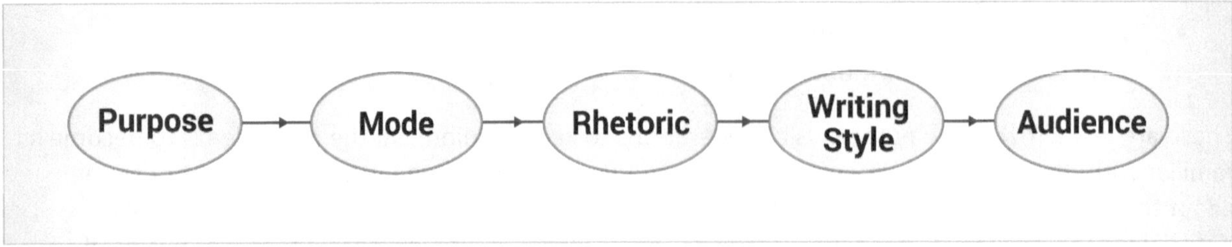

The purpose must pass through these three aspects for effective delivery to the audience. If any elements are not properly considered, the reader will be overly aware of the author, and the message will be lost. The following is a checklist for evaluating the effectiveness of a piece:

- Does the writer choose the appropriate writing mode—argumentative, narrative, descriptive, informative—for his or her purpose?
- Does the writing mode employed contain characteristics inherent to that mode?
- Does the writer consider the personalities/interests/demographics of the intended audience when choosing rhetorical appeals?
- Does the writer use appropriate vocabulary, sentence structure, voice, and tone for the audience demographic?
- Does the author properly establish himself/herself as having authority on the subject, if applicable?
- Does the piece make sense?

Another thing to consider is the medium in which the piece was written. If the medium is a blog, diary, or personal letter, the author may adopt a more casual stance towards the audience. If the piece of writing is a story in a book, a business letter or report, or a published article in a journal or if the task is to gain money or support or to get published, the author may adopt a more formal stance. Ultimately, the writer will want to be very careful in how he or she addresses the reader.

Finally, the effectiveness of a piece can be evaluated by asking how well the purpose was achieved. For example, if students are assigned to read a persuasive essay, instructors can ask whether the author influences students' opinions. Students may be assigned two differing persuasive texts with opposing perspectives and be asked which writer was more convincing. Students can then evaluate what factors contributed to this—for example, whether one author uses more credible supporting facts, appeals more effectively to readers' emotions, presents more believable personal anecdotes, or offers stronger counterargument refutation. Students can then use these evaluations to strengthen their own writing skills.

Level of Detail

Precision

People often think of precision in terms of math, but precise word choice is another key to successful writing. Since language itself is imprecise, it's important for the writer to find the exact word or words to convey the full, intended meaning of a given situation. For example:

> The number of deaths has gone down since seat belt laws started.

There are several problems with this sentence. First, the word *deaths* is too general. From the context, it's assumed that the writer is referring only to deaths caused by car accidents. However, without clarification, the sentence lacks impact and is probably untrue. The phrase "gone down" might be accurate, but a more precise word could provide more information and greater accuracy. Did the numbers show a slow and steady decrease of highway fatalities or a sudden drop? If the latter is true, the writer is missing a chance to make their point more dramatically. Instead of "gone down" they could substitute *plummeted*, *fallen drastically*, or *rapidly diminished* to bring the information to life. Also, the phrase "seat belt laws" is unclear. Does it refer to laws requiring cars to include seat belts or to laws requiring drivers and passengers to use them? Finally, *started* is not a strong verb. Words like *enacted* or *adopted* are more direct and make the content more real. When put together, these changes create a far more powerful sentence:

> The number of highway fatalities has plummeted since laws requiring seat belt usage were enacted.

However, it's important to note that precise word choice can sometimes be taken too far. If the writer of the sentence above takes precision to an extreme, it might result in the following:

The incidence of high-speed, automobile accident-related fatalities has decreased 75% and continued to remain at historical lows since the initial set of federal legislations requiring seat belt use were enacted in 1992.

This sentence is extremely precise, but it takes so long to achieve that precision that it suffers from a lack of clarity. Precise writing is about finding the right balance between information and flow. This is also an issue of conciseness (discussed in the next section).

The last thing to consider with precision is a word choice that's not only unclear or uninteresting, but also confusing or misleading. For example:

The number of highway fatalities has become hugely lower since laws requiring seat belt use were enacted.

In this case, the reader might be confused by the word *hugely*. Huge means large, but here the writer uses *hugely* to describe something small. Though most readers can decipher this, doing so disconnects them from the flow of the writing and makes the writer's point less effective.

Conciseness

"Less is more" is a good rule to follow when writing a sentence. Unfortunately, writers often include extra words and phrases that seem necessary at the time but add nothing to the main idea. This confuses the reader and creates unnecessary repetition. Writing that lacks conciseness is usually guilty of excessive wordiness and redundant phrases. Here's an example containing both of these issues:

> When legislators decided to begin creating legislation making it mandatory for automobile drivers and passengers to make use of seat belts while in cars, a large number of them made those laws for reasons that were political reasons.

There are several empty or "fluff" words here that take up too much space. These can be eliminated while still maintaining the writer's meaning. For example:

- "Decided to begin" could be shortened to "began"
- "Making it mandatory for" could be shortened to "requiring"
- "Make use of" could be shortened to "use"
- "A large number" could be shortened to "many"

In addition, there are several examples of redundancy that can be eliminated:

- "Legislators decided to begin creating legislation" and "made those laws"
- "Automobile drivers and passengers" and "while in cars"
- "Reasons that were political reasons"

These changes are incorporated as follows:

> When legislators began requiring drivers and passengers to use seat belts, many of them did so for political reasons.

There are many general examples of redundant phrases, such as "add an additional," "complete and total," "time schedule," and "transportation vehicle." If asked to identify a redundant phrase on the test, look for words that are close together with the same (or similar) meanings.

Coherence Between Sentences and Paragraphs

Coherence is simply defined as the quality of being logical and consistent. In order to have coherent paragraphs, therefore, authors must be logical and consistent in their writing, whatever the document might be. Two words are helpful to understanding coherence: flow and relationship. Earlier, transitions were referred to as being the "glue" to put organized thoughts together. Now, let's look at the topic sentence from which flow and relationship originate.

The topic sentence, usually the first in a paragraph, holds the essential features that will be brought forth in the paragraph. It is also here that authors either grab or lose readers. It may be the only writing that a reader encounters from that writer, so it is a good idea to summarize and represent ideas accurately.

The coherent paragraph has a logical order. It utilizes transitional words and phrases, parallel sentence structure, clear pronoun references, and reasonable repetition of key words and phrases. Use common sense for repetition. Consider synonyms for variety. Be consistent in verb tense whenever possible.

When writers have accomplished their paragraph's purpose, they prepare it to receive the next paragraph. While writing, read the paragraph over, edit, examine, evaluate, and make changes accordingly. Possibly, a paragraph has gone on too long. If that occurs, it needs to be broken up into other paragraphs, or the length should be reduced. If a paragraph didn't fully accomplish its purpose, consider revising it.

Identifying Details that Develop a Main Idea

The main idea of a piece is the central topic or theme. To identify the main idea, a reader should consider these questions: "What's the point? What does the author want readers to take away from this text?" Everything within the selection should relate back to the main idea because it is the center of the organizational web of any written work. Particularly in articles and reports, the main idea often appears within the opening paragraphs to orient the reader to what the author wants to say about the subject. A sentence that expresses the main idea is known as a thesis sentence or *thesis statement*.

After the main idea has been introduced, *supporting details* are what develop the main idea—they make up the bulk of the work. Without supporting details, the main idea would simply be a statement, so additional details are needed to give that statement weight and validity. Supporting details can often be identified by recognizing the key words that introduce them. The following example offers several supporting details, with key words underlined:

Cheetahs

> Cheetahs are one of the fastest mammals on the land, reaching up to 70 miles an hour over short distances. Even though cheetahs can run as fast as 70 miles an hour, they usually only have to run half that speed to catch up with their choice of prey. Cheetahs cannot maintain a fast pace over long periods of time because their bodies will overheat. After a chase, cheetahs need to rest for approximately 30 minutes prior to eating or returning to any other activity.

In the example, supporting details include:

1. Cheetahs reach up to 70 miles per hour over short distances.
2. They usually only have to run half that speed to catch up with their prey.
3. Cheetahs will overheat if they exert a high speed over longer distances.
4. Cheetahs need to rest for 30 minutes after a chase.

Look at the diagram below (applying the cheetah example) to help determine the hierarchy of topic, main idea, and supporting details.

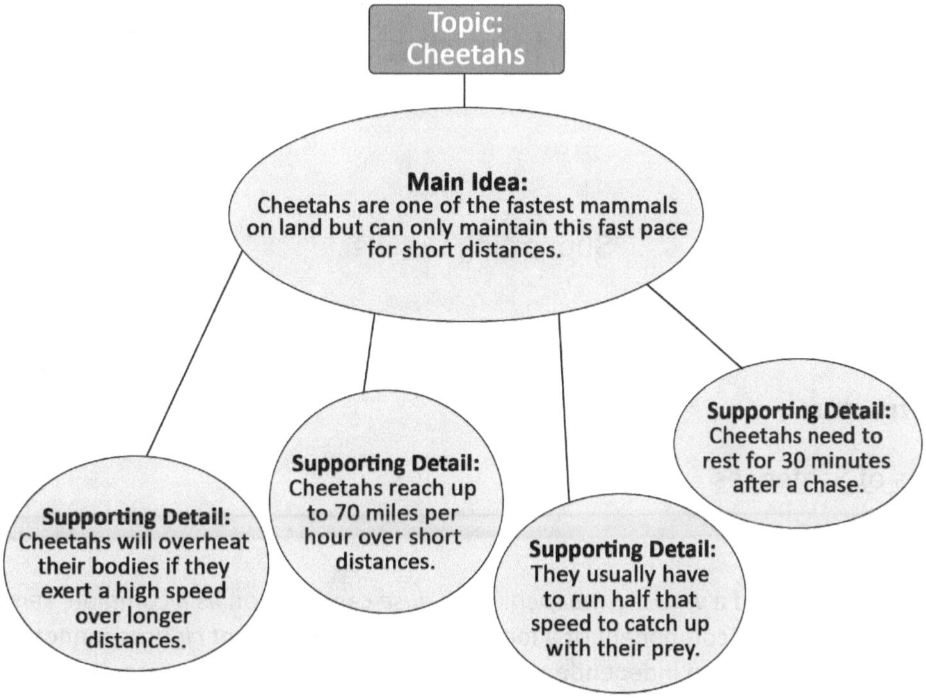

Even though supporting details are more specific than the main idea, they should nevertheless all be directly related to the main idea. Without sufficient supporting details, the writer's main idea will be too weak to be effective.

Organizing a Text Clearly and Coherently

There are five basic elements inherent in effective writing, and each will be discussed throughout the various subheadings of this section.

- *Main idea*: The driving message of the writing, clearly stated or implied
- *Clear organization*: The effective and purposeful arrangement of the content to support the main idea
- *Supporting details/evidence*: Content that gives appropriate depth and weight to the main idea of the story, argument, or information
- *Diction/tone*: The type of language, vocabulary, and word choice used to express the main idea, purposefully aligned to the audience and purpose
- *Adherence to conventions of English*: Correct spelling, grammar, punctuation, and sentence structure, allowing for clear communication of ideas

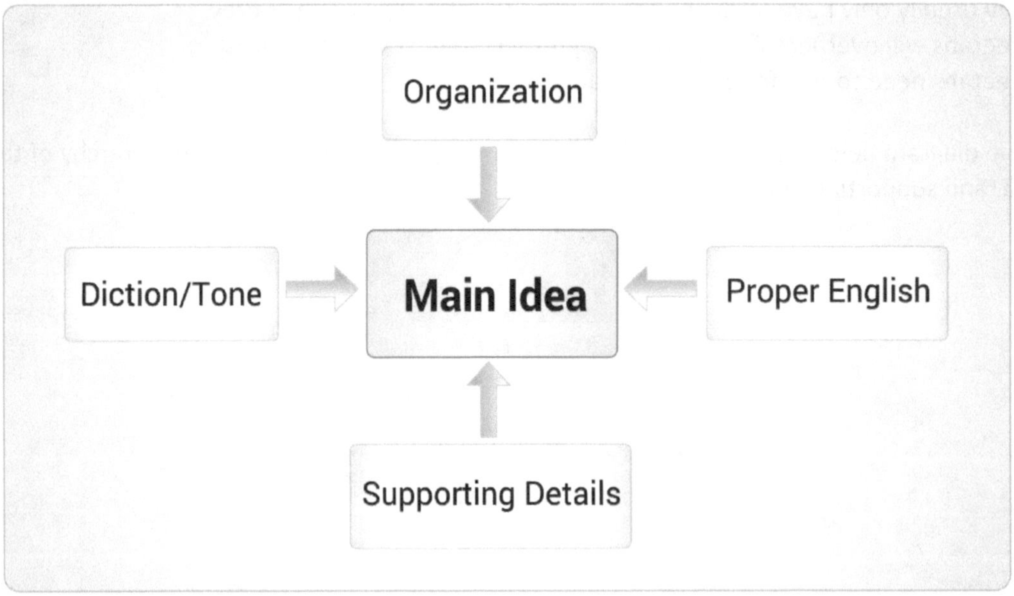

Sentence Structure

Components of Sentences

Clauses

Clauses contain a subject and a verb. An *independent clause* can function as a complete sentence on its own, but it might also be one component of a longer sentence. *Dependent clauses* cannot stand alone as complete sentences. They rely on independent clauses to complete their meaning. Dependent clauses usually begin with a subordinating conjunction. Independent and dependent clauses are sometimes also referred to as *main clauses* and *subordinate clauses*, respectively. The following structure highlights the differences:

> Apiculturists raise honeybees because they love insects.

Apiculturists raise honeybees is an independent or main clause. The subject is *apiculturists*, and the verb is *raise*. It expresses a complete thought and could be a standalone sentence.

Because they love insects is a dependent or subordinate clause. If it were not attached to the independent clause, it would be a sentence fragment. While it contains a subject and verb—*they love*—this clause is dependent because it begins with the subordinate conjunction *because*. Thus, it does not express a complete thought on its own.

Another type of clause is a *relative clause*, and it is sometimes referred to as an *adjective clause* because it gives further description about the noun. A relative clause begins with a *relative pronoun*: *that, which, who, whom, whichever, whomever*, or *whoever.* It may also begin with a *relative adverb*: *where, why*, or *when.* Here's an example of a relative clause, functioning as an adjective:

> The strawberries that I bought yesterday are already beginning to spoil.

Here, the relative clause is *that I bought yesterday*; the relative pronoun is *that*. The subject is *I*, and the verb is *bought*. The clause modifies the subject *strawberries* by answering the question, "Which strawberries?" Here's an example of a relative clause with an adverb:

> The tutoring center is a place where students can get help with homework.

The relative clause is *where students can get help with homework*, and it gives more information about a place by describing what kind of place it is. It begins with the relative adverb *where* and contains the noun *students* along with its verb phrase *can get*.

Relative clauses may be further divided into two types: essential or nonessential. *Essential clauses* contain identifying information without which the sentence would lose significant meaning or not make sense. These are also sometimes referred to as *restrictive clauses*. The sentence above contains an example of an essential relative clause. Here is what happens when the clause is removed:

> The tutoring center is a place where students can get help with homework.
>
> The tutoring center is a place.

Without the relative clause, the sentence loses the majority of its meaning; thus, the clause is essential or restrictive.

Nonessential clauses—also referred to as *non-restrictive clauses*—offer additional information about a noun in the sentence, but they do not significantly control the overall meaning of the sentence. The following example indicates a nonessential clause:

> New York City, which is located in the northeastern part of the country, is the most populated city in America.
>
> New York City is the most populated city in America.

Even without the relative clause, the sentence is still understandable and continues to communicate its central message about New York City. Thus, it is a nonessential clause.

Punctuation differs between essential and nonessential relative clauses, too. Nonessential clauses are set apart from the sentence using commas whereas essential clauses are not separated with commas. Also, the relative pronoun *that* is generally used for essential clauses, while *which* is used for nonessential clauses. The following examples clarify this distinction:

> *Romeo and Juliet* is my favorite play *that Shakespeare wrote*.

The relative clause *that Shakespeare wrote* contains essential, controlling information about the noun *play*, limiting it to those plays by Shakespeare. Without it, it would seem that *Romeo and Juliet* is the speaker's favorite play out of every play ever written, not simply from Shakespeare's repertoire.

> *Romeo and Juliet, which Shakespeare wrote,* is my favorite play.

Here, the nonessential relative clause—"which Shakespeare wrote"—modifies *Romeo and Juliet*. It doesn't provide controlling information about the play, but simply offers further background details. Thus, commas are needed.

Phrases

Phrases are groups of words that do not contain the subject-verb combination required for clauses. Phrases are classified by the part of speech that begins or controls the phrase.

A *noun phrase* consists of a noun and all its modifiers—adjectives, adverbs, and determiners. Noun phrases can serve many functions in a sentence, acting as subjects, objects, and object complements:

> *The shallow yellow bowl* sits on the top shelf.

> Nina just bought *some incredibly fresh organic produce*.

Prepositional phrases are made up of a preposition and its object. The object of a preposition might be a noun, noun phrase, pronoun, or gerund. Prepositional phrases may function as either an adjective or an adverb:

> Jack picked up the book *in front of him*.

The prepositional phrase *in front of him* acts as an adjective indicating which book Jack picked up.

> The dog ran into the back yard.

The phrase *into the backyard* describes where the dog ran, so it acts as an adverb.

Verb phrases include all of the words in a verb group, even if they are not directly adjacent to each other:

> I *should have woken up* earlier this morning.

> The company is now *offering* membership discounts for new enrollers.

This sentence's verb phrase is *is offering*. Even though they are separated by the word *now*, they function together as a single verb phrase.

Structures of Sentences

All sentences contain the same basic elements: a subject and a verb. The *subject* is who or what the sentence is about; the *verb* describes the subject's action or condition. However, these elements, subjects and verbs, can be combined in different ways. The following graphic describes the different types of sentence structures.

Sentence Structure	Independent Clauses	Dependent Clauses
Simple	1	0
Compound	2 or more	0
Complex	1	1 or more
Compound-Complex	2 or more	1 or more

A *simple sentence* expresses a complete thought and consists of one subject and verb combination:

The children ate pizza.

The subject is *children*. The verb is *ate*.

Either the subject or the verb may be *compound*—that is, it could have more than one element:

The children and their parents ate pizza.

The children *ate pizza and watched a movie*.

All of these are still simple sentences. Despite having either compound subjects or compound verbs, each sentence still has only one subject and verb combination.

Compound sentences combine two or more simple sentences to form one sentence that has multiple subject-verb combinations:

The children ate pizza, and *their parents watched a movie*.

This structure is comprised of two independent clauses: (1) *the children ate pizza* and (2) *their parents watched a movie.* Compound sentences join different subject-verb combinations using a comma and a coordinating conjunction.

I called my mom, *but* she didn't answer the phone.

The weather was stormy, *so* we canceled our trip to the beach.

A *complex sentence* consists of an independent clause and one or more dependent clauses. Dependent clauses join a sentence using *subordinating conjunctions*. Some examples of subordinating conjunctions are *although, unless, as soon as, since, while, when, because, if,* and *before*.

I missed class yesterday *because* my mother was ill.

Before traveling to a new country, you need to exchange your money to the local currency.

The order of clauses determines their punctuation. If the dependent clause comes first, it should be separated from the independent clause with a comma. However, if the complex sentence consists of an independent clause followed by a dependent clause, then a comma is not always necessary.

A *compound-complex sentence* can be created by joining two or more independent clauses with at least one dependent clause:

> After the earthquake struck, thousands of homes were destroyed, and many families were left without a place to live.

The first independent clause in the compound structure includes a dependent clause—*after the earthquake struck*. Thus, the structure is both complex and compound.

Main Idea, Thesis Statements, and Topic Sentences

It is very important to know the difference between the topic and the main idea of the text. Even though these two are similar because they both present the central point of a text, they have distinctive differences. A *topic* is the subject of the text; it can usually be described in a one- to two-word phrase and appears in the simplest form. On the other hand, the *main idea* is more detailed and provides the author's central point of the text. It can be expressed through a complete sentence and can be found in the beginning, middle, or end of a paragraph. In most nonfiction books, the first sentence of the passage usually (but not always) states the main idea. Take a look at the passage below to review the topic versus the main idea.

Cheetahs

> Cheetahs are one of the fastest mammals on land, reaching up to 70 miles an hour over short distances. Even though cheetahs can run as fast as 70 miles an hour, they usually only have to run half that speed to catch up with their choice of prey. Cheetahs cannot maintain a fast pace over long periods of time because they will overheat their bodies. After a chase, cheetahs need to rest for approximately 30 minutes prior to eating or returning to any other activity.

In the example above, the topic of the passage is "Cheetahs" simply because that is the subject of the text. The main idea of the text is "Cheetahs are one of the fastest mammals on land but can only maintain this fast pace for short distances." While it covers the topic, it is more detailed and refers to the text in its entirety. The text continues to provide additional details called *supporting details,* which will be discussed in the next section.

Supporting Details

Supporting details help readers better develop and understand the main idea. Supporting details answer questions like *who, what, where, when, why,* and *how*. Different types of supporting details include examples, facts and statistics, anecdotes, and sensory details.

Persuasive and informative texts often use supporting details. In persuasive texts, authors attempt to make readers agree with their point of view, and supporting details are often used as "selling points." If authors make a statement, they should support the statement with evidence in order to adequately persuade readers. Informative texts use supporting details such as examples and facts to inform readers. Take another look at the previous "Cheetahs" passage to find examples of supporting details.

Cheetahs

> Cheetahs are one of the fastest mammals on land, reaching up to 70 miles an hour over short distances. Even though cheetahs can run as fast as 70 miles an hour, they usually only have to run half that speed to catch up with their choice of prey. Cheetahs cannot maintain a fast pace

over long periods of time because they will overheat their bodies. After a chase, cheetahs need to rest for approximately 30 minutes prior to eating or returning to any other activity.

In the example above, supporting details include:

- Cheetahs reach up to 70 miles per hour over short distances.
- They usually only have to run half that speed to catch up with their prey.
- Cheetahs will overheat their bodies if they exert a high speed over longer distances.
- Cheetahs need to rest for 30 minutes after a chase.

Look at the diagram below (applying the cheetah example) to help determine the hierarchy of topic, main idea, and supporting details.

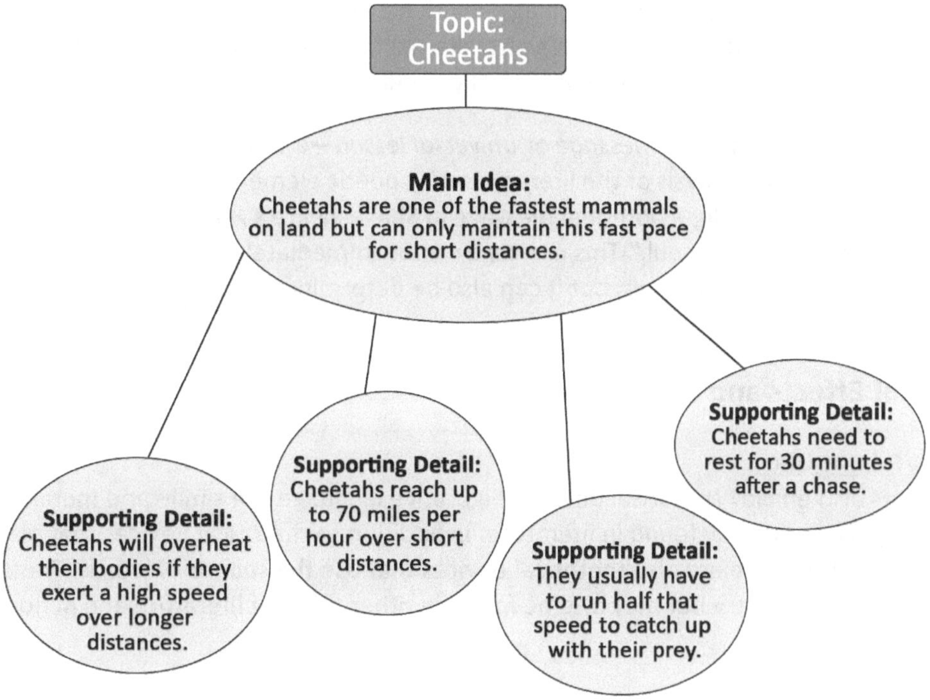

Identifying Theme or Central Message

The *theme* is the central message of a fictional work, whether that work is structured as prose, drama, or poetry. It is the heart of what an author is trying to say to readers through the writing, and theme is largely conveyed through literary elements and techniques.

In literature, a theme can often be determined by considering the over-arching narrative conflict within the work. Though there are several types of conflicts and several potential themes within them, the following are the most common:

- *Individual against the self*—relevant to themes of self-awareness, internal struggles, pride, coming of age, facing reality, fate, free will, vanity, loss of innocence, loneliness, isolation, fulfillment, failure, and disillusionment

- *Individual against nature*— relevant to themes of knowledge vs. ignorance, nature as beauty, quest for discovery, self-preservation, chaos and order, circle of life, death, and destruction of beauty
- *Individual against society*— relevant to themes of power, beauty, good, evil, war, class struggle, totalitarianism, role of men/women, wealth, corruption, change vs. tradition, capitalism, destruction, heroism, injustice, and racism
- *Individual against another individual*— relevant to themes of hope, loss of love or hope, sacrifice, power, revenge, betrayal, and honor

For example, in Hawthorne's *The Scarlet Letter*, one possible narrative conflict could be the individual against the self, with a relevant theme of internal struggles. This theme is alluded to through characterization—Dimmesdale's moral struggle with his love for Hester and Hester's internal struggles with the truth and her daughter, Pearl. It's also alluded to through plot—Dimmesdale's suicide and Hester helping the very townspeople who initially condemned her.

Sometimes, a text can convey a *message* or *universal lesson*—a truth or insight that the reader infers from the text, based on analysis of the literary and/or poetic elements. This message is often presented as a statement. For example, a potential message in Shakespeare's *Hamlet* could be "Revenge is what ultimately drives the human soul." This message can be immediately determined through plot and characterization in numerous ways, but it can also be determined through the setting of Norway, which is bordering on war.

Rhetorical Effects and Emphasis

Figurative Language

Literary texts also employ rhetorical devices. Figurative language like simile and metaphor is a type of rhetorical device commonly found in literature. In addition to rhetorical devices that play on the *meanings* of words, there are also rhetorical devices that use the *sounds* of words. These devices are most often found in poetry but may also be found in other types of literature and in non-fiction writing like speech texts.

Alliteration and *assonance* are both varieties of sound repetition. Other types of sound repetition include: anaphora, repetition that occurs at the beginning of the sentences; epiphora, repetition occurring at the end of phrases; antimetabole, repetition of words in reverse order; and antiphrasis, a form of denial of an assertion in a text.

Alliteration refers to the repetition of the first sound of each word. Recall Robert Burns' opening line:

> My love is like a red, red rose

This line includes two instances of alliteration: "love" and "like" (repeated *L* sound), as well as "red" and "rose" (repeated *R* sound). Next, assonance refers to the repetition of vowel sounds, and can occur anywhere within a word (not just the opening sound). Here is the opening of a poem by John Keats:

> When I have fears that I may cease to be
>
> Before my pen has glean'd my teeming brain

Assonance can be found in the words "fears," "cease," "be," "glean'd," and "teeming," all of which stress the long *E* sound. Both alliteration and assonance create a harmony that unifies the writer's language.

Another sound device is *onomatopoeia*, or words whose spelling mimics the sound they describe. Words such as "crash," "bang," and "sizzle" are all examples of onomatopoeia. Use of onomatopoetic language adds auditory imagery to the text.

Readers are probably most familiar with the technique of *pun*. A pun is a play on words, taking advantage of two words that have the same or similar pronunciation. Puns can be found throughout Shakespeare's plays, for instance:

> Now is the winter of our discontent
> Made glorious summer by this son of York

These lines from *Richard III* contain a play on words. Richard III refers to his brother, the newly crowned King Edward IV, as the "son of York," referencing their family heritage from the house of York. However, while drawing a comparison between the political climate and the weather (times of political trouble were the "winter," but now the new king brings "glorious summer"), Richard's use of the word "son" also implies another word with the same pronunciation, "sun"—so Edward IV is also like the sun, bringing light, warmth, and hope to England. Puns are a clever way for writers to suggest two meanings at once.

Counterarguments

If an author presents a differing opinion or a counterargument in order to refute it, the reader should consider how and why this information is being presented. It is meant to strengthen the original argument and shouldn't be confused with the author's intended conclusion, but it should also be considered in the reader's final evaluation.

Authors can also use bias if they ignore the opposing viewpoint or present their side in an unbalanced way. A strong argument considers the opposition and finds a way to refute it. Critical readers should look for an unfair or one-sided presentation of the argument and be skeptical, as a bias may be present. Even if this bias is unintentional, if it exists in the writing, the reader should be wary of the validity of the argument. Readers should also look for the use of stereotypes, which refer to specific groups. Stereotypes are often negative connotations about a person or place, and should always be avoided. When a critical reader finds stereotypes in a piece of writing, they should be critical of the argument, and consider the validity of anything the author presents. Stereotypes reveal a flaw in the writer's thinking and may suggest a lack of knowledge or understanding about the subject.

Use of Language

There will be many occasions in one's reading career in which an unknown word or a word with multiple meanings will pop up. There are ways of determining what these words or phrases mean that do not require the use of the dictionary, which is especially helpful during a test where one may not be available. Even outside of the exam, knowing how to derive an understanding of a word via context clues will be a critical skill in the real world. The context is the circumstances in which a story or a passage is happening, and can usually be found in the series of words directly before or directly after the word or phrase in question. The clues are the words that hint towards the meaning of the unknown word or phrase.

There may be questions that ask about the meaning of a particular word or phrase within a passage. There are a couple ways to approach these kinds of questions:

1. Define the word or phrase in a way that is easy to comprehend (using context clues).
2. Try out each answer choice in place of the word.

To demonstrate, here's an example from *Alice in Wonderland*:

> Alice was beginning to get very tired of sitting by her sister on the bank, and of having nothing to do: once or twice she peeped into the book her sister was reading, but it had no pictures or conversations in it, "and what is the use of a book," thought Alice, "without pictures or conversations?"
>
> Q: As it is used in the selection, the word peeped means:

Using the first technique, before looking at the answers, define the word "peeped" using context clues and then find the matching answer. Then, analyze the entire passage in order to determine the meaning, not just the surrounding words.

To begin, imagine a blank where the word should be and put a synonym or definition there: "once or twice she ______ into the book her sister was reading." The context clue here is the book. It may be tempting to put "read" where the blank is, but notice the preposition word, "into." One does not read *into* a book, one simply reads a book, and since reading a book requires that it is seen with a pair of eyes, then "look" would make the most sense to put into the blank: "once or twice she looked into the book her sister was reading."

Once an easy-to-understand word or synonym has been supplanted, readers should check to make sure it makes sense with the rest of the passage. What happened after she looked into the book? She thought to herself how a book without pictures or conversations is useless. This situation in its entirety makes sense.

Now check the answer choices for a match:

a. To make a high-pitched cry
b. To smack
c. To look curiously
d. To pout

Since the word was already defined, Choice *C* is the best option.

Using the second technique, replace the figurative blank with each of the answer choices and determine which one is the most appropriate. Remember to look further into the passage to clarify that they work, because they could still make sense out of context.

a. Once or twice she made a high pitched cry into the book her sister was reading
b. Once or twice she smacked into the book her sister was reading
c. Once or twice she looked curiously into the book her sister was reading
d. Once or twice she pouted into the book her sister was reading

For Choice *A*, it does not make much sense in any context for a person to yell into a book, unless maybe something terrible has happened in the story. Given that afterward Alice thinks to herself how useless a book without pictures is, this option does not make sense within context.

For Choice *B*, smacking a book someone is reading may make sense if the rest of the passage indicates a reason for doing so. If Alice was angry or her sister had shoved it in her face, then maybe smacking the book would make sense within context. However, since whatever she does with the book causes her to think, "what is the use of a book without pictures or conversations?" then answer Choice *B* is not an appropriate answer. Answer Choice *C* fits well within context, given her subsequent thoughts on the matter. Answer Choice *D* does not make sense in context or grammatically, as people do not "pout into" things.

This is a simple example to illustrate the techniques outlined above. There may, however, be a question in which all of the definitions are correct and also make sense out of context, in which the appropriate context clues will really need to be honed in on in order to determine the correct answer. For example, here is another passage from *Alice in Wonderland*:

> . . . but when the Rabbit actually took a watch out of its waistcoat pocket, and looked at it, and then hurried on, Alice started to her feet, for it flashed across her mind that she had never before seen a rabbit with either a waistcoat-pocket or a watch to take out of it, and burning with curiosity, she ran across the field after it, and was just in time to see it pop down a large rabbit-hole under the hedge.

Q: As it is used in the passage, the word started means

a. To turn on
b. To begin
c. To move quickly
d. To be surprised

All of these words qualify as a definition of "start," but using context clues, the correct answer can be identified using one of the two techniques above. It's easy to see that one does not turn on, begin, or be surprised to one's feet. The selection also states that she "ran across the field after it," indicating that she was in a hurry. Therefore, to move quickly would make the most sense in this context.

The same strategies can be applied to vocabulary that may be completely unfamiliar. In this case, focus on the words before or after the unknown word in order to determine its definition. Take this sentence, for example:

> Sam was such a miser that he forced Andrew to pay him twelve cents for the candy, even though he had a large inheritance and he knew his friend was poor.

Unlike with assertion questions, for vocabulary questions, it may be necessary to apply some critical thinking skills that may not be explicitly stated within the passage. Think about the implications of the passage, or what the text is trying to say. With this example, it is important to realize that it is considered unusually stingy for a person to demand so little money from someone instead of just letting their friend have the candy, especially if this person is already wealthy. Hence, a miser is a greedy or stingy individual.

Questions about complex vocabulary may not be explicitly asked, but this is a useful skill to know. If there is an unfamiliar word while reading a passage and its definition goes unknown, it is possible to miss out on a critical message that could inhibit the ability to appropriately answer the questions. Practicing this technique in daily life will sharpen this ability to derive meanings from context clues with ease.

Evaluation of Author's Authority and Appeal

Author's Intent

No matter the genre or format, all authors are writing to persuade, inform, entertain, or express feelings. Often, these purposes are blended, with one dominating the rest. It's useful to learn to recognize the author's intent.

Persuasive writing is used to persuade or convince readers of something. It often contains two elements: the argument and the counterargument. The argument takes a stance on an issue, while the counterargument pokes holes in the opposition's stance. Authors rely on logic, emotion, and writer credibility to persuade readers to agree with them. If readers are opposed to the stance before reading, they are unlikely to adopt that stance. However, those who are undecided or committed to the same stance are more likely to agree with the author.

Informative writing tries to teach or inform. Workplace manuals, instructor lessons, statistical reports and cookbooks are examples of informative texts. Informative writing is usually based on facts and is often void of emotion and persuasion. Informative texts generally contain statistics, charts, and graphs. Though most informative texts lack a persuasive agenda, readers must examine the text carefully to determine whether one exists within a given passage.

Stories or narratives are designed to entertain. When you go to the movies, you often want to escape for a few hours, not necessarily to think critically. Entertaining writing is designed to delight and engage the reader. However, sometimes this type of writing can be woven into more serious materials, such as persuasive or informative writing to hook the reader before transitioning into a more scholarly discussion.

Emotional writing works to evoke the reader's feelings, such as anger, euphoria, or sadness. The connection between reader and author is an attempt to cause the reader to share the author's intended emotion or tone. Sometimes in order to make a piece more poignant, the author simply wants readers to feel the same emotions that the author has felt. Other times, the author attempts to persuade or manipulate the reader into adopting his stance. While it's okay to sympathize with the author, be aware of the individual's underlying intent.

How Authors Develop Theme

Authors employ a variety of techniques to present a theme. They may compare or contrast characters, events, places, ideas, or historical or invented settings to speak thematically. They may use analogies, metaphors, similes, allusions, or other literary devices to convey the theme. An author's use of diction, syntax, and tone can also help convey the theme. Authors will often develop themes through the development of characters, use of the setting, repetition of ideas, use of symbols, and through contrasting value systems. Authors of both fiction and nonfiction genres will use a variety of these techniques to develop one or more themes.

Regardless of the literary genre, there are commonalities in how authors, playwrights, and poets develop themes or central ideas.

Authors often do research, the results of which contributes to theme. In prose fiction and drama, this research may include real historical information about the setting the author has chosen or include elements that make fictional characters, settings, and plots seem realistic to the reader. In nonfiction, research is critical since the information contained within this literature must be accurate and, moreover, accurately represented.

In fiction, authors present a narrative conflict that will contribute to the overall theme. In fiction, this conflict may involve the storyline itself and some trouble within characters that needs resolution. In nonfiction, this conflict may be an explanation or commentary on factual people and events.

Authors will sometimes use character motivation to convey theme, such as in the example from *Hamlet* regarding revenge. In fiction, the characters an author creates will think, speak, and act in ways that effectively convey the theme to readers. In nonfiction, the characters are factual, as in a biography, but authors pay particular attention to presenting those motivations to make them clear to readers.

Authors also use literary devices as a means of conveying theme. For example, the use of moon symbolism in Mary Shelley's *Frankenstein* is significant as its phases can be compared to the phases that the Creature undergoes as he struggles with his identity.

The selected point of view can also contribute to a work's theme. The use of first-person point of view in a fiction or non-fiction work engages the reader's response differently than third person point of view. The central idea or theme from a first-person narrative may differ from a third-person limited text.

In literary nonfiction, authors usually identify the purpose of their writing, which differs from fiction, where the general purpose is to entertain. The purpose of nonfiction is usually to inform, persuade, or entertain the audience. The stated purpose of a non-fiction text will drive how the central message or theme, if applicable, is presented.

Authors identify an audience for their writing, which is critical in shaping the theme of the work. For example, the audience for J.K. Rowling's *Harry Potter* series would be different than the audience for a biography of George Washington. The audience an author chooses to address is closely tied to the purpose of the work. The choice of an audience also drives the choice of language and level of diction an author uses. Ultimately, the intended audience determines the level to which that subject matter is presented and the complexity of the theme.

Evaluation of Reasoning

Critical Thinking Skills

It's important to read any piece of writing critically. The goal is to discover the point and purpose of what the author is writing about through analysis. It's also crucial to establish the point or stance the author has taken on the topic of the piece. After determining the author's perspective, readers can then more effectively develop their own viewpoints on the subject of the piece.

It is important to distinguish between *fact and opinion* when reading a piece of writing. A fact is information that can be proven true. If information can be disproved, it is not a fact. For example, water freezes at or below thirty-two degrees Fahrenheit. An argument stating that water freezes at seventy degrees Fahrenheit cannot be supported by data and is therefore not a fact. Facts tend to be associated with science, mathematics, and statistics. Opinions are information open to debate. Opinions are often tied to subjective concepts like equality, morals, and rights. They can also be controversial.

Authors often use words like *think, feel, believe,* or *in my opinion* when expressing opinion, but these words won't always appear in an opinion piece, especially if it is formally written. An author's opinion may be backed up by facts, which gives it more credibility, but that opinion should not be taken as fact.

A critical reader should be suspect of an author's opinion, especially if it is only supported by other opinions.

Fact	Opinion
There are 9 innings in a game of baseball.	Baseball games run too long.
James Garfield was assassinated on July 2, 1881.	James Garfield was a good president.
McDonalds has stores in 118 countries.	McDonalds has the best hamburgers.

Critical readers examine the facts used to support an author's argument. They check the facts against other sources to be sure those facts are correct. They also check the validity of the sources used to be sure those sources are credible, academic, and/or peer-reviewed. Consider that when an author uses another person's opinion to support his or her argument, even if it is an expert's opinion, it is still only an opinion and should not be taken as fact. A strong argument uses valid, measurable facts to support ideas. Even then, the reader may disagree with the argument as it may be rooted in his or her personal beliefs.

An authoritative argument may use the facts to sway the reader. In an example of global warming, many experts differ in their opinions of what alternative fuels can be used to aid in offsetting it. Because of this, a writer may choose to only use the information and expert opinion that supports his or her viewpoint.

If the argument is that wind energy is the best solution, the author will use facts that support this idea. That same author may leave out relevant facts on solar energy. The way the author uses facts can influence the reader, so it's important to consider the facts being used, how those facts are being presented, and what information might be left out.

Critical readers should also look for errors in the argument such as logical fallacies and bias. A *logical fallacy* is a flaw in the logic used to make the argument. Logical fallacies include slippery slope, straw man, and begging the question. Authors can also reflect *bias* if they ignore an opposing viewpoint or present their side in an unbalanced way. A strong argument considers the opposition and finds a way to refute it. Critical readers should look for an unfair or one-sided presentation of the argument and be skeptical, as a bias may be present. Even if this bias is unintentional, if it exists in the writing, the reader should be wary of the validity of the argument.

Readers should also look for the use of *stereotypes,* which refer to specific groups. Stereotypes are often negative connotations about a person or place and should always be avoided. When a critical reader finds stereotypes in a piece of writing, they should immediately be critical of the argument and consider the validity of anything the author presents. Stereotypes reveal a flaw in the writer's thinking and may suggest a lack of knowledge or understanding about the subject.

Identifying False Statements

A reader must also be able to identify any *logical fallacies*—logically flawed statements—that an author may make as those fallacies impact the validity and veracity of the author's claims.

Some of the more common fallacies are shown in the following chart.

Fallacy	Definition
Slippery Slope	A fallacy that is built on the idea that a particular action will lead to a series of events with negative results
Red Herring	The use of an observation or distraction to remove attention from the actual issue
Straw Man	An exaggeration or misrepresentation of an argument so that it is easier to refute
Post Hoc Ergo Propter Hoc	A fallacy that assumes an event to be the consequence of an earlier event merely because it came after it
Bandwagon	A fallacy that assumes because the majority of people feel or believe a certain way then it must be the right way
Ad Hominem	The use of a personal attack on the person or persons associated with a certain argument rather than focusing on the actual argument itself

Readers who are aware of the types of fallacious reasoning are able to weigh the credibility of the author's statements in terms of effective argument. Rhetorical text that contains a myriad of fallacious statements should be considered ineffectual and suspect.

Consistency of Point of View

Point of view is an important writing device to consider. In fiction writing, point of view refers to who tells the story or from whose perspective readers are observing the story. In non-fiction writing, the *point of view* refers to whether the author refers to himself/herself, his/her readers, or chooses not to mention either. Whether fiction or nonfiction, the author will carefully consider the impact the perspective will have on the purpose and main point of the writing.

- *First-person point of view*: The story is told from the writer's perspective. In fiction, this would mean that the main character is also the narrator. First-person point of view is easily recognized by the use of personal pronouns such as *I*, *me*, *we*, *us*, *our*, *my*, and *myself*.
- *Third-person point of view*: In a more formal essay, this would be an appropriate perspective because the focus should be on the subject matter, not the writer or the reader. Third-person

point of view is recognized by the use of the pronouns *he*, *she*, *they*, and *it*. In fiction writing, third-person point of view has a few variations.

- *Third-person limited* point of view refers to a story told by a narrator who has access to the thoughts and feelings of just one character.
- In *third-person omniscient* point of view, the narrator has access to the thoughts and feelings of all the characters.
- In *third-person objective* point of view, the narrator is like a fly on the wall and can see and hear what the characters do and say but does not have access to their thoughts and feelings.

- *Second-person point of view*: This point of view isn't commonly used in fiction or nonfiction writing because it directly addresses the reader using the pronouns *you*, *your*, and *yourself*. Second-person perspective is more appropriate in direct communication, such as business letters or emails.

Point of View	**Pronouns Used**
First person	I, me, we, us, our, my, myself
Second person	You, your, yourself
Third person	He, she, it, they

Transitions

Transitions are the glue that holds the writing together. They function to purposefully incorporate new topics and supporting details in a smooth and coherent way. Usually, transitions are found at the beginnings of sentences, but they can also be located in the middle as a way to link clauses together. There are two types of clauses: independent and dependent as discussed in the language use and vocabulary section.

Transition words connect clauses within and between sentences for smoother writing. "I dislike apples. They taste like garbage." is choppier than "I dislike apples because they taste like garbage." Transitions demonstrate the relationship between ideas, allow for more complex sentence structures, and can alert the reader to which type of organizational format the author is using.

Transition words can be categorized based on the relationships they create between ideas:

- *General order*: signaling elaboration of an idea to emphasize a point—e.g., *for example, for instance, to demonstrate, including, such as, in other words, that is, in fact, also, furthermore, likewise, and, truly, so, surely, certainly, obviously, doubtless*
- *Chronological order*: referencing the time frame in which main event or idea occurs—e.g., *before, after, first, while, soon, shortly thereafter, meanwhile*
- *Numerical order/order of importance*: indicating that related ideas, supporting details, or events will be described in a sequence, possibly in order of importance—e.g., *first, second, also, finally, another, in addition, equally important, less importantly, most significantly, the main reason, last but not least*

- *Spatial order*: referring to the space and location of something or where things are located in relation to each other—e.g., *inside, outside, above, below, within, close, under, over, far, next to, adjacent to*
- *Cause and effect order*: signaling a causal relationship between events or ideas—e.g., *thus, therefore, since, resulted in, for this reason, as a result, consequently, hence, for, so*
- *Compare and contrast order*: identifying the similarities and differences between two or more objects, ideas, or lines of thought—e.g., *like, as, similarly, equally, just as, unlike, however, but, although, conversely, on the other hand, on the contrary*
- *Summary order*: indicating that a particular idea is coming to a close—e.g., *in conclusion, to sum up, in other words, ultimately, above all*

Sophisticated writing also aims to avoid overuse of transitions and ensure that those used are meaningful. Using a variety of transitions makes the writing appear more lively and informed and helps readers follow the progression of ideas.

Sentence-Level Errors

Spelling might or might not be important to some, or maybe it just doesn't come naturally, but those who are willing to discover some new ideas and consider their benefits can learn to spell better and improve their writing. Misspellings reduce a writer's credibility and can create misunderstandings. Spell checkers built into word processors are not a substitute for accuracy. They are neither foolproof nor without error. In addition, a writer's misspelling of one word may also be a word. For example, a writer intending to spell *herd* might accidentally type *s* instead of *d* and unintentionally spell *hers*. Since *hers* is a word, it would not be marked as a misspelling by a spell checker. In short, use spell check, but don't rely on it.

Guidelines for Spelling

Saying and listening to a word serves as the beginning of knowing how to spell it. Keep these subsequent guidelines in mind, remembering there are often exceptions because the English language is replete with them.

Guideline #1: Syllables must have at least one vowel. In fact, every syllable in every English word has a vowel.

- d*o*g
- h*a*yst*a*ck
- *a*nsw*e*r*i*ng
- *a*bst*e*nt*iou*s
- s*i*mpl*e*

Guideline #2: The long and short of it. When the vowel has a short vowel sound as in *mad* or *bed,* only the single vowel is needed. If the word has a long vowel sound, add another vowel, either alongside it or separated by a consonant: bed/*bead*; mad/*made.* When the second vowel is separated by two consonants— *madder*—it does not affect the first vowel's sound.

Guideline #3: Suffixes. Refer to the examples listed below:

- When adding a suffix that starts with a vowel (for example, *-ed*) to a one-syllable root whose vowel has a short sound and ends in a consonant (for example, *stun*), double the final consonant of the root (*n*).

  stun + ed = stun*n*ed

  Exception: If the past tense verb ends in *x* such as *box*, do not double the *x*.

  box + ed = boxed

- If adding a suffix that starts with a vowel (*-er*) to a multi-syllable word ending in a consonant (*begin*), double the consonant (*n*).

  begin + er = begin*n*er

- If a short vowel is followed by two or more consonants in a word such as *i+t+c+h = itch,* do not double the last consonant.

  itch + ed = itched

- If adding a suffix that starts with a vowel (*-ing*) to a word ending in *e* (for example, *name*), that word's final *e* is generally (but not always) dropped.

  name + ing = naming
  exception: manage + able = manageable

- If adding a suffix that starts with a consonant (*-ness*) to a word ending in *e* (*complete*), the *e* generally (but not always) remains.

  complete + ness = completeness
  exception: judge + ment = judgment

- There is great diversity on handling words that end in *y.* For words ending in a vowel + y, nothing changes in the original word.

  play + ed = played

- For words ending in a consonant + *y*, change the *y* to *i* when adding any suffix except for *–ing*.

  marry + ed = married
  marry + ing = marrying

Guideline #4: Which comes first; the *i* or the *e*? Remember the saying, "*I* before *e* except after *c* or when sounding as *a* as in *neighbor* or *weigh*." Keep in mind that these are only guidelines and that there are always exceptions to every rule.

Guideline #5: Vowels in the right order. Another helpful rhyme is, "When two vowels go walking, the first one does the talking." When two vowels are in a row, the first one often has a long vowel sound and the other is silent. An example is *team*.

If you have difficulty spelling words, determine a strategy to help. Work on spelling by playing word games like Scrabble or Words with Friends. Consider using phonics, which is sounding words out by slowly and surely stating each syllable. Try repeating and memorizing spellings as well as picturing words in your head. Try making up silly memory aids. See what works best.

Homophones

Homophones are two or more words that have no particular relationship to one another except their identical pronunciations. Homophones make spelling English words fun and challenging like these:

Common Homophones		
affect, effect	cell, sell	it's, its
allot, a lot	do, due, dew	knew, new
barbecue, barbeque	dual, duel	libel, liable
bite, byte	eminent, imminent	principal, principle
brake, break	flew, flu, flue	their, there, they're
capital, capitol	gauge, gage	to, too, two
cash, cache	holy, wholly	yoke, yolk

Irregular Plurals

Irregular plurals are words that aren't made plural the usual way.

- Most nouns are made plural by adding *–s* (book*s*, television*s*, skyscraper*s*).
- Most nouns ending in *ch, sh, s, x,* or *z* are made plural by adding *–es* (church*es,* marsh*es*).
- Most nouns ending in a vowel + *y* are made plural by adding *–s* (day*s*, toy*s*).
- Most nouns ending in a consonant + *y,* are made plural by the *-y* becoming *-ies* (baby becomes *babies*).
- Most nouns ending in an *o* are made plural by adding *–s* (piano*s,* photo*s*).
- Some nouns ending in an *o*, though, may be made plural by adding *–es* (example: potato*es,* volcano*es*), and, of note, there is no known rhyme or reason for this!
- Most nouns ending in an *f* or *fe* are made plural by the *-f* or *-fe* becoming *-ves*! (example: wolf becomes *wolves*).
- Some words function as both the singular and plural form of the word (fish, deer).
- Other exceptions include *man* becomes *men, mouse* becomes *mice, goose* becomes *geese,* and *foot* becomes *feet.*

Contractions

The basic rule for making *contractions* is one area of spelling that is pretty straightforward: combine the two words by inserting an apostrophe (') in the space where a letter is omitted. For example, to combine *you* and *are*, drop the *a* and put the apostrophe in its place: *you're*.

he + is = he's
you + all = y'all (informal but often misspelled)

Note that *it's*, when spelled with an apostrophe, is always the contraction for *it is*. The possessive form of the word is written without an apostrophe as *its*.

Correcting Misspelled Words

A good place to start looking at commonly misspelled words here is with the word *misspelled*. While it looks peculiar, look at it this way: *mis* (the prefix meaning *wrongly*) + *spelled* = *misspelled*.

Let's look at some commonly misspelled words.

Commonly Misspelled Words					
accept	benign	existence	jewelry	parallel	separate
acceptable	bicycle	experience	judgment	pastime	sergeant
accidentally	brief	extraordinary	library	permissible	similar
accommodate	business	familiar	license	perseverance	supersede
accompany	calendar	February	maintenance	personnel	surprise
acknowledgement	campaign	fiery	maneuver	persuade	symmetry
acquaintance	candidate	finally	mathematics	possess	temperature
acquire	category	forehead	mattress	precede	tragedy
address	cemetery	foreign	millennium	prevalent	transferred
aesthetic	changeable	foremost	miniature	privilege	truly
aisle	committee	forfeit	mischievous	pronunciation	usage
altogether	conceive	glamorous	misspell	protein	valuable
amateur	congratulations	government	mortgage	publicly	vengeance
apparent	courtesy	grateful	necessary	questionnaire	villain
appropriate	deceive	handkerchief	neither	recede	Wednesday
arctic	desperate	harass	nickel	receive	weird
asphalt	discipline	hygiene	niece	recommend	
associate	disappoint	hypocrisy	ninety	referral	
attendance	dissatisfied	ignorance	noticeable	relevant	
auxiliary	eligible	incredible	obedience	restaurant	
available	embarrass	intelligence	occasion	rhetoric	
balloon	especially	intercede	occurrence	rhythm	
believe	exaggerate	interest	omitted	schedule	
beneficial	exceed	irresistible	operate	sentence	

Practice Questions

1. Which of these examples is a compound sentence?
   a. Alex and Shane spent the morning coloring and later took a walk down to the park.
   b. After coloring all morning, Alex and Shane spent the afternoon at the park.
   c. Alex and Shane spent the morning coloring, and then they took a walk down to the park.
   d. After coloring all morning and spending part of the day at the park, Alex and Shane took a nap.

2. Which option best portrays *second person point of view*?
   a. I went down the road, hoping to catch a glimpse of his retreating figure.
   b. You, my dear reader, can understand loss and grief, too.
   c. He left her standing there, alone to face the world.
   d. There's nothing wrong with Margaret.

3. Which phrase below best defines the term *audience* as it is used in rhetoric?
   a. The group of readers to which the author is trying to appeal
   b. Students
   c. Subject matter experts
   d. Readers who already have formed subject matter opinions

4. Which of the following refers to what an author wants to express about a given subject?
   a. Primary purpose
   b. Plot
   c. Main idea
   d. Characterization

5. Which organizational style is used in the following passage?

   There are several reasons why the new student café has not been as successful as expected. One factor is that prices are higher than originally advertised, so many students cannot afford to buy food and beverages there. Also, the café closes rather early; as a result, students go out in town to other late-night gathering places rather than meeting friends at the café on campus.

   a. Cause and effect order
   b. Compare and contrast order
   c. Spatial order
   d. Time order

Answer Explanations

1. C: Choice *C* is a compound sentence because it joins two independent clauses with a comma and the coordinating conjunction *and*. The sentences in Choices B and D include one independent clause and one dependent clause, so they are complex sentences, not compound sentences. The sentence in Choice *A* has both a compound subject, *Alex and Shane*, and a compound verb, *spent and took*, but the entire sentence itself is one independent clause.

2. B: The correct answer is *B* as the author is speaking directly to the reader and uses the pronoun *you*. Choice *A* uses first person point of view, which uses the pronoun *I*. Choice *C* uses third person point of view which utilizes pronouns such as *he*, *she*, or *we*. Choice *D* is unclear.

3. A: The correct answer is the group of readers to which the author is trying to appeal. Choice *B* could be a partial answer, but it is incorrect. Choice *C* assumes authors only write for experts, so it is incorrect. Choice *D* is not true. Rhetoric tries to appeal to readers and tries to convince them of a thesis.

4. C: The main idea of a piece is its central theme or subject and what the author wants readers to know or understand after they read. Choice *A* is incorrect because the primary purpose is the reason that a piece was written, and while the main idea is an important part of the primary purpose, the above elements are not developed with that intent. Choice *B* is incorrect because while the plot refers to the events that occur in a narrative, organization, tone, and supporting details are not used only to develop plot. Choice *D* is incorrect because characterization is the description of a person.

5. A: The passage describes a situation and then explains the causes that led to it. Also, it utilizes cause and effect signal words, such as *causes, factors, so,* and *as a result*. *B* is incorrect because a compare and contrast order considers the similarities and differences of two or more things. *C* is incorrect because spatial order describes where things are located in relation to each other. Finally, *D* is incorrect because time order describes when things occurred chronologically.

Ability to Use Source Materials

Use of Reference Materials

Reference materials are indispensable tools for beginners and experts alike. Becoming a competent English communicator doesn't necessarily mean memorizing every single rule about spelling, grammar, or punctuation—it means knowing where and how to find accurate information about the rules of English usage. Students of English have a wide variety of references materials available to them, and, in an increasingly digitized world, more and more of these materials can be found online or as easily-accessible phone applications. Educators should introduce students to different types of reference materials as well as when and how to use them.

Spell Check

Most word processing software programs come equipped with a spell-checking feature. Web browsers and personal devices like smartphones and tablets may also have a spell checker enabled. *Spell check* automatically detects misspelled words and suggests alternate spellings. Many writers have come to rely on spell check due to its convenience and ease of use. However, there are some caveats to using spell check—it only checks whether a word is spelled correctly, not if it is used correctly. As discussed above, there are numerous examples of commonly-confused words in English, the misuse of which may not be detected by a spell checker. Many word processing programs do integrate spell checking and grammar checking functions, however. Thus, although running a spell check is an important part of reviewing any piece of writing, it should not be the only step of the review process. Further, spell checkers recommend correctly-spelled words based on an approximation of the misspelled word, so writers need to be somewhat close to the correct spelling in order for spell check to be useful.

Dictionary

Dictionaries are readily available in print, digital formats, and as mobile apps. A dictionary offers a wealth of information to users. First, in the absence of spell checking software, a *dictionary* can be used to identify correct spelling and to determine the word's pronunciation—often written using the International Phonetic Alphabet (IPA). Perhaps the best-known feature of a dictionary is its explanation of a word's meanings, as a single word can have multiple definitions. A dictionary organizes these definitions based on their parts of speech and then arranges them from most to least commonly used meanings or from oldest to most modern usage. Many dictionaries also offer information about a word's etymology and usage. With all these functions, then, a dictionary is a basic, essential tool in many situations. Students can turn to a dictionary when they encounter an unfamiliar word or when they see a familiar word used in a new way.

There are many dictionaries to choose from, but perhaps the most highly respected source is the *Oxford English Dictionary* (OED). The OED is a historical dictionary, and as such, all entries include quotes of the word as it has been used throughout history. Users of the OED can get a deeper sense of a word's evolution over time and in different parts of the world. Another standard dictionary in America is *Merriam-Webster*.

Thesaurus

Whereas a dictionary entry lists a word's definitions, a *thesaurus* entry lists a word's *synonyms* and *antonyms*—i.e., words with similar and opposite meanings, respectively. A dictionary can be used to find out what a word means and where it came from, and a thesaurus can be used to understand a word's relationship to other words. A thesaurus can be a powerful vocabulary-building tool. By becoming familiar with synonyms and antonyms, students will be more equipped to use a broad range of vocabulary in their speech and writing. Of course, one thing to be aware of when using a thesaurus is that most words do not have exact synonyms. Rather, there are slight nuances of meaning that can make one word more appropriate than another in a given context. In this case, it is often to the user's advantage to consult a thesaurus side-by-side with a dictionary to confirm any differences in usage between two synonyms. Some digital sources, such as *Dictionary.com*, integrate a dictionary and a thesaurus.

Generally, though, a thesaurus is a useful tool to help writers add variety and precision to their word choice. Consulting a thesaurus can help students elevate their writing to an appropriate academic level by replacing vague or overused words with more expressive or academic ones. Also, word processors often offer a built-in thesaurus, making it easy for writers to look up synonyms and vary word choice as they work.

Glossary

A *glossary* is similar to a dictionary in that it offers an explanation of terms. However, while a dictionary attempts to cover every word in a language, a glossary only focuses on those terms relevant to a specific field. Also, a glossary entry is more likely to offer a longer explanation of a term and its relevance within that field. Glossaries are often found at the back of textbooks or other nonfiction publications in order to explain new or unfamiliar terms to readers. A glossary may also be an entire book on its own that covers all of the essential terms and concepts within a particular profession, field, or other specialized area of knowledge. For learners seeking general definitions of terms from any context, then, a dictionary is an appropriate reference source, but for students of specialized fields, a glossary will usually provide more in-depth information.

Style Manual

Many rules of English usage are standard, but other rules may be more subjective. An example can be seen in the following structures:

A. I went to the store and bought eggs, milk, and bread.
B. I went to the store and bought eggs, milk and bread.

The final comma in a list before *and* or *or* is known as an Oxford comma or serial comma. It is, recommended in some styles, but not in others. To determine the appropriate use of the Oxford comma, writers can consult a style manual.

A *style manual* is a comprehensive collection of guidelines for language use and document formatting. Some fields refer to a common style guide—e.g., the Associated Press or *AP Stylebook*, a standard in American journalism. Individual organizations may rely on their own house style. Regardless, the purpose of a style manual is to ensure uniformity across all documents. Style manuals explain things such as how to format titles, when to write out numbers or use numerals, and how to cite sources. Because there are many different style guides, students should know how and when to consult an appropriate guide. The Chicago Manual of Style is common in the publication of books and academic journals. The Modern Language Association style (MLA) is another commonly used academic style format, while the American Psychological Association style (APA) may be used for scientific publications. Familiarity with using a style guide is particularly important for students who are college bound or pursuing careers in academic or professional writing.

In the examples above, the Oxford comma is recommended by the Chicago Manual of Style, so sentence A would be correct if the writer is using this style. But the comma is not recommended by the *AP Stylebook*, so sentence B would be correct if the writer is using the AP style.

General Grammar and Style References

Any language arts textbook should offer general grammatical and stylistic advice to students, but there are a few well-respected texts that can also be used for reference. *Elements of Style* by William Strunk is regularly assigned to students as a guide on effective written communication, including how to avoid common usage mistakes and how to make the most of parallel structure. *Garner's Modern American Usage* by Bryan Garner is another text that guides students on how to achieve precision and understandability in their writing. Whereas other reference sources discussed above tend to address specific language concerns, these types of texts offer a more holistic approach to cultivating effective language skills.

Electronic Resources

With print texts, it is easy to identify the authors and their credentials, as well as the publisher and their reputation. With electronic resources like websites, though, it can be trickier to assess the reliability of information. Students should be alert when gathering information from the Internet. Understanding the significance of website *domains*—which include identification strings of a site—can help. Website domains ending in *.edu* are educational sites and tend to offer more reliable research in their field. A *.org* ending tends to be used by nonprofit organizations and other community groups, *.com* indicates a privately-owned website, and a *.gov* site is run by the government. Websites affiliated with official organizations, research groups, or institutes of learning are more likely to offer relevant, fact-checked, and reliable information.

Evaluation of Sources

Identifying Relevant Information During Research

Relevant information is that which is pertinent to the topic at hand. Particularly when doing research online, it is easy for students to get overwhelmed with the wealth of information available to them. Before conducting research, then, students need to begin with a clear idea of the question they want to answer.

For example, a student may be interested in learning more about marriage practices in Jane Austen's England. If that student types "marriage" into a search engine, he or she will have to sift through thousands of unrelated sites before finding anything related to that topic. Narrowing down search parameters can aid in locating relevant information.

When using a book, students can consult the table of contents, glossary, or index to discover whether the book contains relevant information before using it as a resource. If the student finds a hefty volume on Jane Austen, he or she can flip to the index in the back, look for the word marriage, and find out how many page references are listed in the book. If there are few or no references to the subject, it is probably not a relevant or useful source.

In evaluating research articles, students may also consult the title, abstract, and keywords before reading the article in its entirety. Referring to the date of publication will also determine whether the research contains up-to-date discoveries, theories, and ideas about the subject, or whether it is outdated.

Evaluating the Credibility of a Print or Digital Source

There are several additional criteria that need to be examined before using a source for a research topic.

The following questions will help determine whether a source is credible:

- Author
    - Who is he or she?
    - Does he or she have the appropriate credentials—e.g., M.D, PhD?
    - Is this person authorized to write on the matter through his/her job or personal experiences?
    - Is he or she affiliated with any known credible individuals or organizations?
    - Has he or she written anything else?
- Publisher
    - Who published/produced the work? Is it a well-known journal, like National Geographic, or a tabloid, like The National Enquirer?
    - Is the publisher from a scholarly, commercial, or government association?
    - Do they publish works related to specific fields?
    - Have they published other works?
    - If a digital source, what kind of website hosts the text? Does it end in .edu, .org, or .com?
- Bias
    - Is the writing objective? Does it contain any loaded or emotional language?
    - Does the publisher/producer have a known bias, such as Fox News or CNN?
    - Does the work include diverse opinions or perspectives?
    - Does the author have any known bias—e.g., Michael Moore, Bill O'Reilly, or the Pope? Is he or she affiliated with any organizations or individuals that may have a known bias—e.g., Citizens United or the National Rifle Association?
    - Does the magazine, book, journal, or website contain any advertising?
- References
    - Are there any references?
    - Are the references credible? Do they follow the same criteria as stated above?
    - Are the references from a related field?
- Accuracy/reliability
    - Has the article, book, or digital source been peer reviewed?
    - Are all of the conclusions, supporting details, or ideas backed with published evidence?
    - If a digital source, is it free of grammatical errors, poor spelling, and improper English?
    - Do other published individuals have similar findings?
- Coverage
    - Are the topic and related material both successfully addressed?
    - Does the work add new information or theories to those of their sources?
    - Is the target audience appropriate for the intended purpose?

Integration of Resource Material

It can be daunting to integrate so many sources into a research paper while still maintaining fluency and coherency. Most source material is incorporated in the form of quotations or paraphrases, while citing the source at the end of their respective references.

There are several guidelines to consider when integrating a source into writing:

- The piece should be written in the author's voice. Quotations, especially long ones, should be limited and spaced evenly throughout the paper.
- All paragraphs should begin with the author's own words and end with his or her own words; quotations should never start or end a paragraph.
- Quotations and paraphrases should be used to emphasize a point, give weight to an idea, and validate a claim.
- Supporting evidence should be introduced in a sentence or paragraph, and then explained afterwards: *According to Waters (1979)* [signal phrase], *"All in all, we're just another brick in the wall" (p.24). The wall suggests that people are becoming more alienated, and the bricks symbolize a paradoxical connection to that alienation* [Explanation].
- When introducing a source for the first time, the author's name and a smooth transition should be included: *In Pink Floyd's groundbreaking album The Wall, Roger Waters argues that society is causing people to become more alienated.*
- There should be an even balance between quotations and paraphrases.
- Quotations or paraphrases should never be taken out of context in a way that alters the original author's intent.
- Quotations should be syntactically and grammatically integrated.
- Quotations should not simply be copied and pasted in the paper, rather, they should be introduced into a paper with natural transitions.
    - As argued in Johnson's article…
    - Evidence of this point can be found in Johnson's article, where she asserts that…
    - The central argument of John's article is…

Documentation of Sources

Identifying the Components of a Citation

Citation styles vary according to which style guide is consulted. Examples of commonly-used styles include MLA, APA, and Chicago/Turabian. Each citation style includes similar components, although the order and formatting of these components varies.

MLA Style

For an MLA style citation, components must be included or excluded depending on the source, so writers should determine which components are applicable to the source being cited. Here are the basic components:

- Author—last name, first name
- Title of source
- Title of container—e.g., a journal title or website
- Other contributors—e.g., editor or translator
- Version
- Number
- Publisher
- Publication date
- Location—e.g., the URL or DOI
- Date of Access—optional

APA Style

The following components can be found in APA style citations. Components must be included or excluded depending on the source, so writers should determine which components are applicable to the source being cited.

The basic components are as follows:

- Author—last name, first initial, middle initial
- Publication date
- Title of chapter, article, or text
- Editor— last name, first initial, middle initial
- Version/volume
- Number/issue
- Page numbers
- DOI or URL
- Database—if article is difficult to locate
- City of publication
- State of publication, abbreviated
- Publisher

Chicago/Turabian Style

Chicago/Turabian style citations are also referred to as note systems and are used most frequently in the humanities and the arts. Components must be included or excluded depending on the source, so writers should determine which components are applicable to the source being cited. They contain the following elements:

- Author—last name, first name, middle initial
- Title of chapter or article—in quotation marks
- Title of source
- Editor—first name, last name
- Page numbers
- Version/volume
- Number/issue
- Page numbers
- Date of access
- DOI
- Publication location—city and state abbreviation/country
- Publisher
- Publication Date

Citing Source Material Appropriately

The following information contains examples of the common types of sources used in research as well as the formats for each citation style. First lines of citation entries are presented flush to the left margin, and second/subsequent details are presented with a hanging indent. Some examples of bibliography entries are presented below:

Book

- MLA
  Format: Last name, First name, Middle initial. *Title of Source*. Publisher, Publication Date.
  Example: Sampson, Maximus R. *Diaries from an Alien Invasion*. Campbell Press, 1989.
- APA
  Format: Last name, First initial, Middle initial. (Year Published) *Book Title.* City, State: Publisher.
  Example: Sampson, M. R. (1989). *Diaries from an Alien Invasion. Springfield, IL*: Campbell Press.
- Chicago/Turabian
  Format: Last name, First name, Middle initial. *Book Title*. City, State: Publisher, Year of publication.
  Example: Sampson, Maximus R. *Diaries from an Alien Invasion. Springfield, IL*: Campbell Press, 1989.

A Chapter in an Edited Book

- MLA
  Format: Last name, First name, Middle initial. "Title of Source." *Title of Container*, Other Contributors, Publisher, Publication Date, Location.
  Example: Sampson, Maximus R. "The Spaceship." *Diaries from an Alien Invasion*, edited by Allegra M. Brewer, Campbell Press, 1989, pp. 45-62.

- APA
  Format: Last name, First Initial, Middle initial. (Year Published) Chapter title. In First initial, Middle initial, Last Name (Ed.), *Book title* (pp. page numbers). City, State: Publisher.
  Example: Sampson, M. R. (1989). The Spaceship. In A. M. Brewer (Ed.), *Diaries from an Alien Invasion* (pp. 45-62). Springfield, IL: Campbell Press.
- Chicago/Turabian
  Format: Last name, First name, Middle initial. "Chapter Title." In Book Title, edited by Editor's Name (First, Middle In. Last), Page(s). City: Publisher, Year Published.
  Example: Sampson, Maximus R. "The Spaceship," in *Diaries from an Alien Invasion*, edited by Allegra M. Brewer, 45-62. Springfield: Campbell Press, 1989.

Article in a Journal

- MLA
  Format: Last name, First name, Middle initial. "Title of Source." *Title of Journal, Number, Publication* Date, Location.
  Example: Rowe, Jason R. "The Grief Monster." *Strong Living*, vol. 9, no. 9, 2016, pp 25-31.
- APA
  Format: Last name, First initial, Middle initial. (Year Published). Title of article. *Name of Journal, volume*(issue), page(s).
  Example: Rowe, J. R. (2016). The grief monster. *Strong Living, 9*(9), 25-31.
- Chicago/Turabian:
  Format: Last name, First name, Middle initial. "Title of Article." *Name of Journal* volume, issue (Year Published): Page(s).
  Example: Rowe, Jason, R. "The Grief Monster." *Strong Living* 9, no. 9 (2016): 25-31.

Page on a Website

- MLA
  Format: Last name, First name, Middle initial. "Title of Article." *Name of Website*, date published (Day Month Year), URL. Date accessed (Day Month Year).
  Example: Rowe, Jason. "The Grief Monster." *Strong Living Online*, 9 Sept. 2016. http://www.somanylosses.com/the-grief-monster/html. Accessed 13 Sept. 2016.
- APA
  Format: Last name, First initial. Middle initial. (Date Published—Year, Month Day). Page or article title. Retrieved from URL
  Example: Rowe, J. W. (2016, Sept. 9). The grief monster. Retrieved from http://www.somanylosses.com/ the-grief-monster/html
- Chicago/Turabian
  Format: Last Name, First Name, Middle initial. "Page Title." *Website Title*. Last modified Month day, year. Accessed month, day, year. URL.
  Example: Rowe, Jason. "The Grief Monster." Strong Living Online. Last modified September 9, 2016. Accessed September 13, 2016. http://www.somanylosses.com/the-grief-monster/html.

In-Text Citations

Most of the content found in a research paper will be supporting evidence that must be cited in-text, i.e., directly after the sentence that makes the statement. In-text citations contain details that correspond to the first detail in the bibliography entry—usually the author.

- MLA style - In-text citations will contain the author and the page number (if the source has page numbers) for direct quotations. Paraphrased source material may have just the author.
  - According to Johnson, liver cancer treatment is "just beyond our reach" (976).
  - The treatment of liver cancer is not within our reach, currently (Johnson).
  - The narrator opens the story with a paradoxical description: "It was the best of times, it was the worst of times" (Dickens 1).
- APA Style - In text citations will contain the author, the year of publication, and a page marker—if the source is paginated—for direct quotations. Paraphrased source material will include the author and year of publication.
  - According to Johnson (1986), liver cancer treatment is "just beyond our reach" (p. 976).
  - The treatment of liver cancer is not within our reach, currently (Johnson, 1986).
- Chicago Style - Chicago style has two approaches to in-text citation: notes and bibliography or author-date.
  - Notes – There are two options for notes: endnotes—provided in a sequential list at the end of the paper and separate from bibliography—or footnotes provided at the bottom of a page. In either case, the use of superscript indicates the citation number.
    - Johnson states that treatment of liver cancer is "just beyond our reach." [1]
    - 1. Robert W. Johnson, Oncology in the Twenty-first Century (Kentville, Nova Scotia: Kentville Publishing, 1986), 159.
  - Author-Date – The author-date system includes the author's name, publication year, and page number.
    - Johnson states that treatment of liver cancer is "just beyond our reach" (1986, 159).

Practice Questions

1. A student encounters the word *aficionado* and wants to learn more about it. It doesn't sound like other English words he knows, so the student is curious to identify the word's origin. What resource should he consult?
    a. A thesaurus
    b. A dictionary
    c. A style guide
    d. A grammar book

2. Which domain is likely to be used by a website run by a nonprofit group?
    a. .com
    b. .edu
    c. .org
    d. .gov

3. Which of the following should be evaluated to ensure the credibility of a source?
    a. The publisher, the author, and the references
    b. The subject, the title, and the audience
    c. The organization, stylistic choices, and transition words
    d. The length, the tone, and the contributions of multiple authors

4. Which of the following is true of using citations in a research paper?
    a. If a source is cited in the bibliography, it is not necessary to cite it in the paper as well.
    b. In-text citations differ in format from bibliographic citations.
    c. Students should learn one standard method of citing sources.
    d. Books and articles need to be cited, but not websites or multimedia sources.

5. Which of the following is true regarding the integration of source material to maintain the flow of ideas in a research project or paper?
    a. There should be at least one quotation or paraphrase in every paragraph.
    b. If a source is paraphrased instead of being directly quoted, it is not necessary to include a citation.
    c. An author's full name must be used in every signal phrase.
    d. In-text citations should be used to support the paper's argument without overwhelming the student's writing.

Answer Explanations

1. B: A word's origin is also known as its *etymology*. In addition to offering a detailed list of a word's various meanings, a dictionary also provides information about a word's history, such as when it first came into use, what language it originated from, and how its meaning may have changed over time. A thesaurus is for identifying synonyms and antonyms, so *A* is incorrect. A style guide provides formatting, punctuation, and syntactical advice for a specific field, and a grammar book is related to the appropriate placement of words and punctuation, which does not provide any insight into a word's meaning. Therefore, Choices *A*, *C*, and *D* are incorrect.

2. C: The .org domain on websites is generally used by nonprofit groups or community organizations. A government website uses .gov, and .edu is used for educational institutions. Private companies and businesses use .com, so Choices *A*, *B*, and *D* are incorrect.

3. A: The publisher, author, and references are elements of a resource that determine credibility. If the publisher has published more than one work, the author has written more than one piece on the subject, or the work references other recognized research, the credibility of a source will be stronger. Choice *B* is incorrect because the subject and title may be used to determine relevancy, not credibility, and the audience does not have much to do with the credibility of a source. Choice *C* is incorrect because the organization, stylistic choices, and transition words are all components of an effectively-written piece, but they have less to do with credibility, other than to ensure that the author knows how to write. The length and tone of a piece are a matter of author's preference, and a work does not have to be written by multiple people to be considered a credible source.

4. B: In-text citations are much shorter and usually only include the author's last name, page numbers being referenced, and for some styles, the publication year. Bibliographic citations contain much more detailed reference information. *B* is incorrect because citations are necessary both in the text and in a bibliography. *C* is incorrect because there are several different citation styles depending on the type of paper or article being written. Rather, students should learn when it is appropriate to apply each different style. *D* is incorrect because all sources need to be cited regardless of medium.

5. D: The purpose of integrating research is to add support and credibility to the student's ideas, not to replace the student's own ideas altogether. Choice *A* is incorrect as the bulk of the paper or project should be comprised of the author's own words, and quotations and paraphrases should be used to support them. Outside sources should be included when they enhance the writer's argument, but they are not required in every single paragraph. Choice *B* is also incorrect because regardless of whether ideas are directly quoted or paraphrased, it is essential to always credit authors for their ideas. The use of the author's full name in every signal phrase is unnecessary, so Choice *C* is also incorrect.

Rhetorical Analysis

Appeals

In non-fiction writing, authors employ argumentative techniques to present their opinion to readers in the most convincing way. Persuasive writing usually includes at least one type of appeal: an appeal to logic (logos), emotion (pathos), or credibility and trustworthiness (ethos). When a writer appeals to logic, they are asking readers to agree with them based on research, evidence, and an established line of reasoning. An author's argument might also appeal to readers' emotions, perhaps by including personal stories and anecdotes (a short narrative of a specific event). A final type of appeal, appeal to authority, asks the reader to agree with the author's argument on the basis of their expertise or credentials. Consider three different approaches to arguing the same opinion:

- Logic (Logos)

  Our school should abolish its current ban on cell phone use on campus. This rule was adopted last year as an attempt to reduce class disruptions and help students focus more on their lessons. However, since the rule was enacted, there has been no change in the number of disciplinary problems in class. Therefore, the rule is ineffective and should be done away with.

  The above is an example of an appeal to logic. The author uses evidence to disprove the logic of the school's rule (the rule was supposed to reduce discipline problems, but the number of problems has not been reduced; therefore, the rule is not working) and call for its repeal.

- Emotion (Pathos)

  An author's argument might also appeal to readers' emotions, perhaps by including personal stories and anecdotes.

  The next example presents an appeal to emotion. By sharing the personal anecdote of one student and speaking about emotional topics like family relationships, the author invokes the reader's empathy in asking them to reconsider the school rule.

  > Our school should abolish its current ban on cell phone use on campus. If they aren't able to use their phones during the school day, many students feel isolated from their loved ones. For example, last semester, one student's grandmother had a heart attack in the morning. However, because he couldn't use his cell phone, the student didn't know about his grandmother's accident until the end of the day—when she had already passed away, and it was too late to say goodbye. By preventing students from contacting their friends and family, our school is placing undue stress and anxiety on students.

- Credibility (Ethos)

  Finally, an appeal to authority includes a statement from a relevant expert. In this case, the author uses a doctor in the field of education to support the argument. All three examples begin from the same opinion—the school's phone ban needs to change—but rely on different argumentative styles to persuade the reader.

  > Our school should abolish its current ban on cell phone use on campus. According to Dr. Bartholomew Everett, a leading educational expert, "Research studies show that cell phone usage has no real impact on student attentiveness. Rather, phones provide a valuable technological resource for learning. Schools need to learn how to integrate this new technology into their curriculum." Rather than banning phones altogether, our school should follow the advice of experts and allow students to use phones as part of their learning.

Rhetorical Questions

Another commonly used argumentative technique is asking rhetorical questions, questions that do not actually require an answer but that push the reader to consider the topic further.

> I wholly disagree with the proposal to ban restaurants from serving foods with high sugar and sodium contents. Do we really want to live in a world where the government can control what we eat? I prefer to make my own food choices.

Here, the author's rhetorical question prompts readers to put themselves in a hypothetical situation and imagine how they would feel about it.

Tone

Tone refers to the writer's attitude toward the subject matter. Tone is usually explained in terms of a work of fiction. For example, the tone conveys how the writer feels about their characters and the situations in which they're involved. Nonfiction writing is sometimes thought to have no tone at all; however, this is incorrect.

A lot of nonfiction writing has a neutral tone, which is an important tone for the writer to take. A neutral tone demonstrates that the writer is presenting a topic impartially and letting the information speak for itself. On the other hand, nonfiction writing can be just as effective and appropriate if the tone isn't neutral. For instance, take this example involving seat belts:

> Seat belts save more lives than any other automobile safety feature. Many studies show that airbags save lives as well; however, not all cars have airbags. For instance, some older cars don't. Furthermore, air bags aren't entirely reliable. For example, studies show that in 15% of accidents airbags don't deploy as designed, but, on the other hand, seat belt malfunctions are extremely rare. The number of highway fatalities has plummeted since laws requiring seat belt usage were enacted.

In this passage, the writer mostly chooses to retain a neutral tone when presenting information. If the writer would instead include their own personal experience of losing a friend or family member in a car accident, the tone would change dramatically. The tone would no longer be neutral and would show that the writer has a personal stake in the content, allowing them to interpret the information in a different way. When analyzing tone, consider what the writer is trying to achieve in the text and how they *create* the tone using style.

Organization/Structure

Writing can be classified under four passage types: narrative, expository, descriptive (sometimes called technical), and persuasive. Though these types are not mutually exclusive, one form tends to dominate the rest. By recognizing the *type* of passage you're reading, you gain insight into *how* you should read. If you're reading a narrative, you can assume the author intends to entertain, which means you may skim the text without losing meaning. A technical document might require a close read because skimming the passage might cause the reader to miss salient details.

1. *Narrative* writing, at its core, is the art of storytelling. For a narrative to exist, certain elements must be present. First, it must have characters. While many characters are human, characters could be defined as anything that thinks, acts, and talks like a human. For example, many recent movies, such as *Lord of the Rings* and *The Chronicles of Narnia*, include animals, fantastical creatures, and even trees that behave like humans. Second, it must have a plot or sequence of events. Typically, those events follow a standard plot diagram, but recent trends start *in medias res* or in the middle (near the climax). In this instance, foreshadowing and flashbacks often fill in plot details. Finally, along with characters and a plot, there must also be conflict. Conflict is usually divided into two types: internal and external. Internal conflict indicates the character is in turmoil and is presented through the character's thoughts. External conflicts are visible. Types of external conflict include a person versus nature, another person, or society.

2. *Expository* writing is detached and to the point. Since expository writing is designed to instruct or inform, it usually involves directions and steps written in second person ("you" voice) and lacks any persuasive or narrative elements. Sequence words such as *first*, *second*, and *third*, or *in the first place*, *secondly*, and *lastly* are often given to add fluency and cohesion. Common examples of expository writing include instructor's lessons, cookbook recipes, and repair manuals.

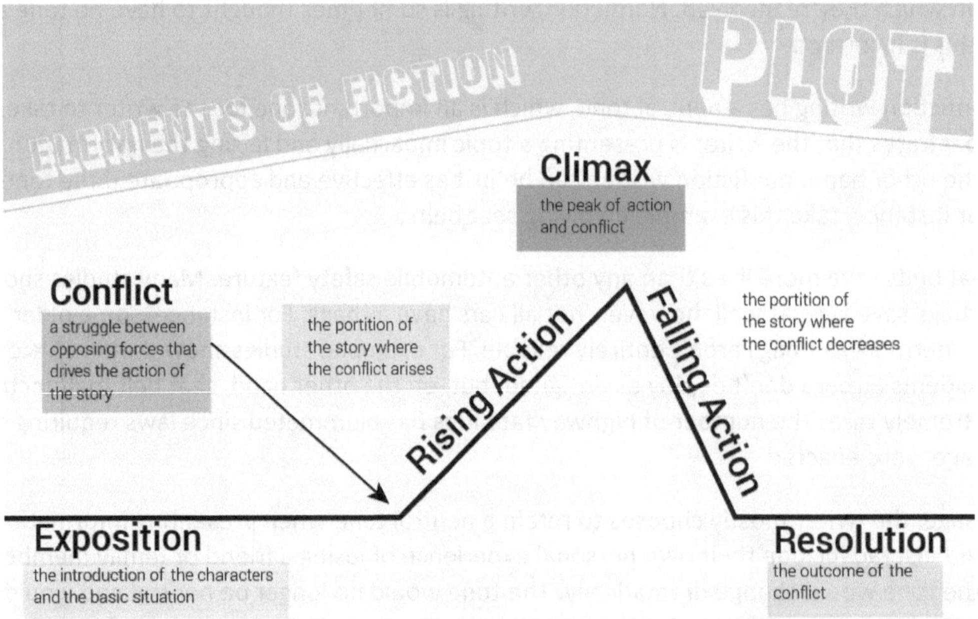

3. Due to its empirical nature, *technical* writing is filled with steps, charts, graphs, data, and statistics. The goal of technical writing is to advance understanding in a field through the scientific method. Experts such as teachers, doctors, or mechanics use words unique to the profession in which they operate. These words, which often incorporate acronyms, are called *jargon*. Technical writing is a type of expository writing but is not meant to be understood by the general public. Instead, technical writers assume readers have received a formal education in a particular field of study and need no explanation as to what the jargon means. Imagine a doctor trying to understand a diagnostic reading for a car or a mechanic trying to interpret lab results. Only professionals with proper training will fully comprehend the text.

4. *Persuasive* writing is designed to change opinions and attitudes. The topic, stance, and arguments are found in the thesis, positioned near the end of the introduction. Later supporting paragraphs offer relevant quotations, paraphrases, and summaries from primary or secondary sources, which are then interpreted, analyzed, and evaluated. The goal of persuasive writers is not to stack quotes but to develop original ideas by using sources as a starting point. Good persuasive writing makes powerful arguments with valid sources and thoughtful analysis. Poor persuasive writing is riddled with bias and logical fallacies. Sometimes logical and illogical arguments are sandwiched together in the same piece. Therefore, readers should display skepticism when reading persuasive arguments.

Rhetorical Effects

A *rhetorical device* is the phrasing and presentation of an idea that reinforces and emphasizes a point in an argument. A rhetorical device is often quite memorable. One of the more famous uses of a rhetorical device is in John F. Kennedy's 1961 inaugural address: "Ask not what your country can do for you, ask what you can do for your country." The contrast of ideas presented in the phrasing is an example of the rhetorical device of antimetabole. Some other common examples are provided below, but test takers should be aware that this is not a complete list.

Device	Definition	Example
Allusion	A reference to a famous person, event, or significant literary text as a form of significant comparison	"We are apt to shut our eyes against a painful truth, and listen to the song of that siren till she transforms us into beasts." Patrick Henry
Anaphora	The repetition of the same words at the beginning of successive words, phrases, or clauses, designed to emphasize an idea	"We shall not flag or fail. We shall go on to the end. We shall fight in France, we shall fight on the seas and oceans, we shall fight with growing confidence ... we shall fight in the fields and in the streets, we shall fight in the hills. We shall never surrender." Winston Churchill

Device	Definition	Example
Understatement	A statement meant to portray a situation as less important than it actually is to create an ironic effect	"The war in the Pacific has not necessarily developed in Japan's favor." Emperor Hirohito, surrendering Japan in World War II
Parallelism	A syntactical similarity in a structure or series of structures used for impact of an idea, making it memorable	"A penny saved is a penny earned." Ben Franklin
Rhetorical question	A question posed that is not answered by the writer though there is a desired response, most often designed to emphasize a point	"Can anyone look at our reduced standing in the world today and say, 'Let's have four more years of this?'" Ronald Reagan

Use of Language

Making Inferences

Readers should be able to make *inferences*. Making an inference requires the reader to read between the lines and look for what is *implied* rather than what is directly stated. That is, using information that is known from the text, the reader is able to make a logical assumption about information that is *not* directly stated but is probably true. Read the following passage:

> "Hey, do you wanna meet my new puppy?" Jonathan asked.
>
> "Oh, I'm sorry but please don't—" Jacinta began to protest, but before she could finish, Jonathan had already opened the passenger side door of his car and a perfect white ball of fur came bouncing towards Jacinta.
>
> "Isn't he the cutest?" beamed Jonathan.
>
> "Yes—achoo!—he's pretty—aaaachooo!!—adora—aaa—aaaachoo!" Jacinta managed to say in between sneezes. "But if you don't mind, I—I—achoo!—need to go inside."

Which of the following can be inferred from Jacinta's reaction to the puppy?

a. she hates animals
b. she is allergic to dogs
c. she prefers cats to dogs
d. she is angry at Jonathan

An inference requires the reader to consider the information presented and then form their own idea about what is probably true. Based on the details in the passage, what is the best answer to the question? Important details to pay attention to include the tone of Jacinta's dialogue, which is overall polite and apologetic, as well as her reaction itself, which is a long string of sneezes. Answer choices (a) and (d) both express strong emotions ("hates" and "angry") that are not evident in Jacinta's speech or actions. Answer choice (c) mentions cats, but there is nothing in the passage to indicate Jacinta's feelings about cats. Answer choice (b), "she is allergic to dogs," is the most logical choice—based on the fact that she began sneezing as soon as a fluffy dog approached her, it makes sense to guess that Jacinta might be allergic to dogs. So even though Jacinta never directly states, "Sorry, I'm allergic to dogs!" using the clues in the passage, it is still reasonable to guess that this is true.

Making inferences is crucial for readers of literature because literary texts often avoid presenting complete and direct information to readers about characters' thoughts or feelings, or they present this information in an unclear way, leaving it up to the reader to interpret clues given in the text. In order to make inferences while reading, readers should ask themselves:

- What details are being presented in the text?
- Is there any important information that seems to be missing?
- Based on the information that the author *does* include, what else is probably true?
- Is this inference reasonable based on what is already known?

Apply Information

A natural extension of being able to make an inference from a given set of information is also being able to apply that information to a new context. This is especially useful in non-fiction or informative writing. Considering the facts and details presented in the text, readers should consider how the same information might be relevant in a different situation. The following is an example of applying an inferential conclusion to a different context:

> Often, individuals behave differently in large groups than they do as individuals. One example of this is the psychological phenomenon known as the bystander effect. According to the bystander effect, the more people who witness an accident or crime occur, the less likely each individual bystander is to respond or offer assistance to the victim. A classic example of this is the murder of Kitty Genovese in New York City in the 1960s. Although there were over thirty witnesses to her killing by a stabber, none of them intervened to help Kitty or contact the police.

Considering the phenomenon of the bystander effect, what would probably happen if somebody tripped on the stairs in a crowded subway station?

a. Everybody would stop to help the person who tripped
b. Bystanders would point and laugh at the person who tripped
c. Someone would call the police after walking away from the station
d. Few if any bystanders would offer assistance to the person who tripped

This question asks readers to apply the information they learned from the passage, which is an informative paragraph about the bystander effect. According to the passage, this is a concept in psychology that describes the way people in groups respond to an accident—the more people are present, the less likely any one person is to intervene. While the passage illustrates this effect with the example of a woman's murder, the question asks readers to apply it to a different context—in this case, someone falling down the stairs in front of many subway passengers. Although this specific situation is not discussed in the passage, readers should be able to apply the general concepts described in the paragraph. The definition of the bystander effect includes any instance of an accident or crime in front of a large group of people. The question asks about a situation that falls within the same definition, so the general concept should still hold true: in the midst of a large crowd, few individuals are likely to actually respond to an accident. In this case, answer choice (d) is the best response.

Evaluation of Evidence

Analyzing and Evaluating Text Structure

Depending on what the author is attempting to accomplish, certain formats or text structures work better than others. For example, a sequence structure might work for narration but not when identifying similarities and differences between dissimilar concepts. Similarly, a comparison-contrast structure is not useful for narration. It's the author's job to put the right information in the correct format.

Readers should be familiar with these main literary structures:

1. *Sequence* structure (sometimes referred to as the order structure) is when the order of events proceed in a predictable order. In many cases, this means the text goes through the plot elements: exposition, rising action, climax, falling action, and resolution. Readers are introduced to characters, setting, and conflict in the exposition. In the rising action, there's an increase in tension and suspense. The climax is the height of tension and the point of no return. Tension decreases during the falling action. In the resolution, any conflicts presented in the exposition are solved, and the story concludes. An informative text that is structured sequentially will often go in order from one step to the next.

2. In the *problem-solution* structure, authors identify a potential problem and suggest a solution. This form of writing is usually divided into two paragraphs and can be found in informational texts. For example, cell phone, cable, and satellite providers use this structure in manuals to help customers troubleshoot or identify problems with services or products.

3. When authors want to discuss similarities and differences between separate concepts, they arrange thoughts in a *comparison-contrast* paragraph structure. Venn diagrams are an effective graphic organizer for comparison-contrast structures because they feature two overlapping circles that can be used to organize similarities and differences. A comparison-contrast essay organizes one paragraph based on similarities and another based on differences. A comparison-contrast essay can also be arranged with the similarities and differences of individual traits addressed within individual paragraphs. Words such as *however*, *but*, and *nevertheless* help signal a contrast in ideas.

4. *Descriptive* writing structure is designed to appeal to your senses. Much like an artist who constructs a painting, good descriptive writing builds an image in the reader's mind by appealing to the five senses: sight, hearing, taste, touch, and smell. However, overly descriptive writing can become tedious; whereas sparse descriptions can make settings and characters seem flat. Good authors strike a balance by applying descriptions only to passages, characters, and settings that are integral to the plot.

5. Passages that use the *cause and effect* structure are simply asking *why* by demonstrating some type of connection between ideas. Words such as *if*, *since*, *because*, *then*, or *consequently* indicate relationship. By switching the order of a complex sentence, the writer can rearrange the emphasis on different clauses. Saying *If Sheryl is late, we'll miss the dance* is different from saying *We'll miss the dance if Sheryl is late*. One emphasizes Sheryl's tardiness while the other

emphasizes missing the dance. Paragraphs can also be arranged in a cause and effect format. Since the format—before and after—is sequential, it is useful when authors wish to discuss the impact of choices. Researchers often apply this paragraph structure to the scientific method.

6. Texts presented in *chronological order* are stories that occur within a specific time and setting. Within this time setting, they do not jump around time or place, but one event happens after the other the way it would in reality. Chronological order is similar to sequence structure; however, the difference is that sequence structure does not have to occur at a specific time or place, and chronological order does.

7. An additional way to structure a text is by stating the *conclusion* first, and then adding the *premises* or *arguments* after the conclusion is stated. This structure is best used if you believe your audience is going to be receptive to your argument. If they are, you can go ahead and state your opinion to get them interested and on board. Authors will follow their conclusion with the appropriate supporting details and arguments in order to solidify their claim.

Text Evidence

Text evidence is the information readers find in a text or passage that supports the main idea or point(s) in a story. In turn, text evidence can help readers draw conclusions about the text or passage. The information should be taken directly from the text or passage and placed in quotation marks. Text evidence provides readers with information to support ideas about the text so that they do not rely simply on their own thoughts. Details should be precise, descriptive, and factual. Statistics are a great piece of text evidence because they provide readers with exact numbers and not just a generalization. For example, instead of saying "Asia has a larger population than Europe," authors could provide detailed information such as, "In Asia there are over 4 billion people, whereas in Europe there are a little over 750 million." More definitive information provides better evidence to readers to help support their conclusions about texts or passages.

Text Credibility

Credible sources are important when drawing conclusions because readers need to be able to trust what they are reading. Authors should always use credible sources to help gain the trust of their readers. A text is *credible* when it is believable and the author is objective and unbiased. If readers do not trust an author's words, they may simply dismiss the text completely. For example, if an author writes a persuasive essay, he or she is outwardly trying to sway readers' opinions to align with his or her own. Readers may agree or disagree with the author, which may, in turn, lead them to believe that the author is credible or not credible. Also, readers should keep in mind the source of the text. If readers review a journal about astronomy, would a more reliable source be a NASA employee or a medical doctor? Overall, text credibility is important when drawing conclusions because readers want reliable sources that support the decisions they have made about the author's ideas.

Examining Paragraphs

While authors write, thoughts coalesce to form words on "paper" (aka a computer screen). Authors strategically place those thoughts in sentences to give them "voice" in an orderly manner, and then they manipulate them into cohesive sentences for cohesion to express ideas. Like a hunk of modeling clay (thanks to computers, people are no longer bound to erasers and whiteout), sentences can be worked and reworked until they cooperate and say what was originally intended.

Before calling a paragraph complete, identify its main point, making sure that related sentences stay on point. Pose questions such as, "Did I sufficiently develop the main point? Did I say it succinctly enough? Did I give it time to develop? *Is* it developed?"

Let's examine the following two paragraphs, each an example of a movie review. Read them and form a critique.

> Example 1: *Eddie the Eagle* is a movie about a struggling athlete. Eddie was crippled at birth. He had a lot of therapy and he had a dream. Eddie trained himself for the Olympics. He went far away to learn how to ski jump. It was hard for him, but he persevered. He got a coach and kept trying. He qualified for the Olympics. He was the only one from Britain who could jump. When he succeeded, they named him, "Eddie the Eagle."

> Example 2: The last movie I saw in the theater was *Eddie the Eagle,* a story of extraordinary perseverance inspired by real life events. Eddie was born in England with a birth defect that he slowly but surely overcame, but not without trial and error (not the least of which was his father's perpetual *dis*couragement). In fact, the old man did everything to get him to give up, but Eddie was dogged beyond anyone in the neighborhood; in fact, maybe beyond anyone in the whole town or even the whole world! Eddie, simply, did not know to quit. As he grew up, so did his dream; a strange one, indeed, for someone so unaccomplished: to compete in the Winter Olympics as a ski jumper (which he knew absolutely nothing about). Eddie didn't just keep on dreaming about it. He actually went to Germany and *worked* at it, facing unbelievable odds, defeats, and put-downs by Dad and the other Men in Charge, aka the Olympic decision-makers. Did that stop him? No way! Eddie got a coach and persevered. Then, when he failed, he persevered some more, again and again. You should be able to open up a dictionary, look at the word "persevere," and see a picture of Eddie the Eagle because, when everybody told him he couldn't, he did. The result? He is forever dubbed, "Eddie the Eagle."

Both reviews tell something about the movie *Eddie the Eagle*. Does one motivate the reader to want to see the movie more than the other? Does one just provide a few facts while the other paints a virtual picture of the movie? Does one give a carrot and the other a rib eye steak, mashed potatoes, and chocolate silk pie?

Paragraphs sometimes only give facts. Sometimes that's appropriate and all that is needed. Sometimes, though, writers want to use the blank documents on their computer screens to paint a picture. Writers must "see" the painting come to life. To do so, pick a familiar topic, write a simple sentence, and add to it. Pretend, for instance, there's a lovely view. What does one see? Is it a lake? Try again – picture it as though it were the sea! Visualize a big ship sailing out there. Is it sailing away or approaching? Who is on it? Is it dangerous? Is it night and are there crazy pirates on board? Uh-oh! Did one just jump ship and start swimming toward shore?

Summarizing

At the end of a text or passage, it is important to summarize what the readers read. Summarizing is a strategy in which readers determine what is important throughout the text or passage, shorten those ideas, and rewrite or retell it in their own words. A summary should identify the main idea of the text or passage. Important details or supportive evidence should also be accurately reported in the summary. If writers provide irrelevant details in the summary, it may cloud the greater meaning of the summary in the text. When summarizing, writers should not include their opinions, quotes, or what they thought the author should have said. A clear summary provides clarity of the text or passage to the readers. Let's review the checklist of items writers should include in their summary.

Summary Checklist

- Title of the story
- Someone: Who is or are the main character(s)?
- Wanted: What did the character(s) want?
- But: What was the problem?
- So: How did the character(s) solve the problem?
- Then: How did the story end? What was the resolution?

Paraphrasing

Another strategy readers can use to help them fully comprehend a text or passage is paraphrasing. Paraphrasing is when readers take the author's words and put them into their own words. When readers and writers paraphrase, they should avoid copying the text—that is plagiarism. It is also important to include as many details as possible when restating the facts. Not only will this help readers and writers recall information, but by putting the information into their own words, they demonstrate whether or not they fully comprehend the text or passage. Look at the example below showing an original text and how to paraphrase it.

> *Original Text*: Fenway Park is home to the beloved Boston Red Sox. The stadium opened on April 20, 1912. The stadium currently seats over 37,000 fans, many of whom travel from all over the country to experience the iconic team and nostalgia of Fenway Park.
>
> *Paraphrased*: On April 20, 1912, Fenway Park opened. Home to the Boston Red Sox, the stadium now seats over 37,000 fans. Many spectators travel to watch the Red Sox and experience the spirit of Fenway Park.

Paraphrasing, summarizing, and quoting can often cross paths with one another. Review the chart below showing the similarities and differences between the three strategies.

Paraphrasing	Summarizing	Quoting
Uses own words	Puts main ideas into own words	Uses words that are identical to text
References original source	References original source	Requires quotation marks
Uses own sentences	Shows important ideas of source	Uses author's own words and ideas

Directly Stated Information Versus Implications

Engaged readers should constantly self-question while reviewing texts to help them form conclusions. Self-questioning is when readers review a paragraph, page, passage, or chapter and ask themselves, "Did I understand what I read?," "What was the main event in this section?," "Where is this taking place?," and so on. Authors can provide clues or pieces of evidence throughout a text or passage to guide readers toward a conclusion. This is why active and engaged readers should read the text or passage in its entirety before forming a definitive conclusion. If readers do not gather all the pieces of evidence needed, then they may jump to an illogical conclusion.

At times, authors directly state conclusions while others simply imply them. Of course, it is easier if authors outwardly provide conclusions to readers because it does not leave any information open to interpretation. On the other hand, implications are things that authors do not directly state but can be assumed based off of information they provided. If authors only imply what may have happened, readers can form a menagerie of ideas for conclusions. For example, look at the following statement: "Once we heard the sirens, we hunkered down in the storm shelter." In this statement, the author does not directly state that there was a tornado, but clues such as "sirens" and "storm shelter" provide insight to the readers to help form that conclusion.

Practice Questions

1. Which phrase below best defines *inference*?
   a. Reading between the lines
   b. Skimming a text for context clues
   c. Writing notes or questions that need answers during the reading experience
   d. Summarizing the text

2. Which mode of writing aims to inform the reader objectively about a particular subject or idea and typically contains definitions, instructions, or facts within its subject matter?
   a. Argumentative
   b. Informative
   c. Narrative
   d. Descriptive

3. The rhetorical appeal that elicits an emotional and/or sympathetic response from an audience is known as which of the following?
   a. Logos
   b. Ethos
   c. Pathos
   d. None of the above

4. Which of the following describes the organizational pattern of chronological or sequence order?
   a. Text organized by describing a dilemma and a possible solution
   b. Text organized by observing the consequences of an action
   c. Text organized by the timing of events or actions
   d. Text organized by analyzing the relative placement of an object or event

The next question is based on the following passage.

A famous children's author recently published a historical fiction novel under a pseudonym; however, it did not sell as many copies as her children's books. In her earlier years, she had majored in history and earned a graduate degree in Antebellum American History, which is the time frame of her new novel. Critics praised this newest work far more than the children's series that made her famous. In fact, her new novel was nominated for the prestigious Albert J. Beveridge Award but still isn't selling like her children's books, which fly off the shelves because of her name alone.

5. Which one of the following statements might be accurately inferred based on the above passage?
   a. The famous children's author produced an inferior book under her pseudonym.
   b. The famous children's author is the foremost expert on Antebellum America.
   c. The famous children's author did not receive the bump in publicity for her historical novel that it would have received if it were written under her given name.
   d. People generally prefer to read children's series than historical fiction.

Answer Explanations

1. A: Inferring is reading between the lines. Choice *B* describes the skimming technique. Choice *C* describes a questioning technique readers should employ, and Choice *D* is a simple statement regarding summary. It's an incomplete answer and not applicable to inference.

2. B: The key word here is "inform," which is the primary purpose of all informative modes. They contain facts, definitions, instructions, and other elements with the objective purpose of informing a reader—such as study guides, instruction manuals, and textbooks. Choice *A* is incorrect because an argumentative mode contains language that is subjective and is intended to persuade or to inform with a persuasive bias. Choice *C* is incorrect as a narrative mode is used primarily to tell a story and has no intention of informing, nor is the language inherently objective. Choice *D* is incorrect as descriptive modes possess no inherent intent to inform, and are used primarily to describe.

3. C: Pathos is the rhetorical appeal that draws on an audience's emotions and sympathies. Choice *A* is incorrect as logos appeals to the audience's logic, reason, and rational thinking, using facts and definitions. Choice *B* is incorrect because ethos appeals to the audience's sense of ethics and moral obligations. Choice *D* is incorrect because *C* contains the correct answer; thus, the answer cannot be "None of the above."

4. C: The correct answer is text organized by the timing of events or actions. Chronological or sequence order is the organizational pattern that structures text to show the passage of time or movement through steps in a certain order. Choice *A* demonstrates the problem/solution structure. Choice *B* defines the cause/effect pattern. Choice *D* represents the spatial order structure.

5. C: We are looking for an inference—a conclusion that is reached on the basis of evidence and reasoning—from the passage that will likely explain why the famous children's author did not achieve her usual success with the new genre (despite the book's acclaim). Choice *A* is wrong because the statement is false according to the passage. Choice *B* is wrong because, although the passage says the author has a graduate degree on the subject, it would be an unrealistic leap to infer that she is the foremost expert on Antebellum America. Choice *D* is wrong because there is nothing in the passage to lead us to infer that people generally prefer a children's series to historical fiction. In contrast, Choice *C* can be logically inferred since the passage speaks of the great success of the children's series and the declaration that the fame of the author's name causes the children's books to "fly off the shelves." Thus, she did not receive any bump from her name since she published the historical novel under a pseudonym, which makes Choice *C* correct.

The Essays

Directions

On the first essay in the CLEP, you will have thirty minutes to write an essay discussing to what extent you agree or disagree on the statement provided. On the second essay, you will have forty minutes to write an essay after reading two sources. The second essay involves practice in synthesizing text. Synthesizing text means taking multiple texts and drawing conclusions from the information provided in them.

Brainstorming

One of the most important steps in writing an essay is prewriting. Before drafting an essay, it's helpful to think about the topic for a moment or two, in order to gain a more solid understanding of what the task is. Then, spending about five minutes jotting down the immediate ideas that could work for the essay is recommended. It is a way to get some words on the page and offer a reference for ideas when drafting. Scratch paper is provided for writers to use any prewriting techniques such as webbing, free writing, or listing. The goal is to get ideas out of the mind and onto the page.

Considering Opposing Viewpoints

In the planning stage, it's important to consider all aspects of the topic, including different viewpoints on the subject. There are more than two ways to look at a topic, and a strong argument considers those opposing viewpoints. Considering opposing viewpoints can help writers present a fair, balanced, and informed essay that shows consideration for all readers. This approach can also strengthen an argument by recognizing and potentially refuting the opposing viewpoint(s).

Drawing from personal experience may help to support ideas. For example, if the goal for writing is a personal narrative, then the story should be from the writer's own life. Many writers find it helpful to draw from personal experience, even in an essay that is not strictly narrative. Personal anecdotes or short stories can help to illustrate a point in other types of essays as well.

Moving from Brainstorming to Planning

Once the ideas are on the page, it's time to turn them into a solid plan for the essay. The best ideas from the brainstorming results can then be developed into a more formal outline. An outline typically has one main point (the thesis) and at least three sub-points that support the main point. Here's an example:

Main Idea

- Point #1
- Point #2
- Point #3

Of course, there will be details under each point, but this approach is the best for dealing with timed writing.

Staying on Track

Basing the essay on the outline aids in both organization and coherence. The goal is to ensure that there is enough time to develop each sub-point in the essay, roughly spending an equal amount of time on each idea. Keeping an eye on the time will help. If there are fifteen minutes left to draft the essay, then it makes sense to spend about 5 minutes on each of the ideas. Staying on task is critical to success, and timing out the parts of the essay can help writers avoid feeling overwhelmed.

Parts of the Essay

The *introduction* has to do a few important things:

- Establish the *topic* of the essay in original wording (i.e., not just repeating the prompt)
- Clarify the significance/importance of the topic or purpose for writing (not too many details, a brief overview)
- Offer a *thesis statement* that identifies the writer's own viewpoint on the topic (typically one-two brief sentences as a clear, concise explanation of the main point on the topic)

Body paragraphs reflect the ideas developed in the outline. Three-four points is probably sufficient for a short essay, and they should include the following:

- A *topic sentence* that identifies the sub-point (e.g., a reason why, a way how, a cause or effect)
- A detailed *explanation* of the point, explaining why the writer thinks this point is valid
- Illustrative examples, such as personal examples or real-world examples, that support and validate the point (i.e., "prove" the point)
- A *concluding sentence* that connects the examples, reasoning, and analysis to the point being made

The *conclusion*, or final paragraph, should be brief and should reiterate the focus, clarifying why the discussion is significant or important. It is important to avoid adding specific details or new ideas to this paragraph. The purpose of the conclusion is to sum up what has been said to bring the discussion to a close.

Don't Panic!

Writing an essay can be overwhelming, and performance panic is a natural response. The outline serves as a basis for the writing and helps to keep writers focused. Getting stuck can also happen, and it's helpful to remember that brainstorming can be done at any time during the writing process. Following the steps of the writing process is the best defense against writer's block.

Timed essays can be particularly stressful, but assessors are trained to recognize the necessary planning and thinking for these timed efforts. Using the plan above and sticking to it helps with time management. Timing each part of the process helps writers stay on track. Sometimes writers try to cover too much in their essays. If time seems to be running out, this is an opportunity to determine whether all of the ideas in the outline are necessary. Three body paragraphs are sufficient, and more than that is probably too much to cover in a short essay.

More isn't always *better* in writing. A strong essay will be clear and concise. It will avoid unnecessary or repetitive details. It is better to have a concise, five-paragraph essay that makes a clear point, than a ten-paragraph essay that doesn't. The goal is to write one-two pages of quality writing. Paragraphs should also reflect balance; if the introduction goes to the bottom of the first page, the writing may be going off-track or be repetitive. It's best to fall into the one-two page range, but a complete, well-developed essay is the ultimate goal.

The Final Steps

Leaving a few minutes at the end to revise and proofread offers an opportunity for writers to polish things up. Putting one's self in the reader's shoes and focusing on what the essay actually says helps writers identify problems—it's a movement from the mindset of writer to the mindset of editor. The goal is to have a clean, clear copy of the essay. The following areas should be considered when proofreading:

- Sentence fragments
- Awkward sentence structure
- Run-on sentences
- Incorrect word choice
- Grammatical agreement errors
- Spelling errors
- Punctuation errors
- Capitalization errors

The Short Overview

The essay may seem challenging, but following these steps can help writers focus:

- Take one-two minutes to think about the topic.
- Generate some ideas through brainstorming (three-four minutes).
- Organize ideas into a brief outline, selecting just three-four main points to cover in the essay (eventually the body paragraphs).
- Develop essay in parts:
- Introduction paragraph, with intro to topic and main points
- Viewpoint on the subject at the end of the introduction
- Body paragraphs, based on outline
- Each paragraph: makes a main point, explains the viewpoint, uses examples to support the point
- Brief conclusion highlighting the main points and closing
- Read over the essay (last five minutes).
- Look for any obvious errors, making sure that the writing makes sense.

Practice Test

Conventions of Standard Written English

The following sentences test skills of grammar and usage. Some sentences will contain no error, and the rest will contain only one error.

1.(A) An important issues stemming (B) from this meeting is that (C) we won't have enough time (D) to meet all of the objectives. (E) No error

2. (A) The rising popularity of the clean-eating movement (B) attributing to the fact that experts say added (C) sugars and chemicals in our food (D) are to blame for the obesity epidemic. (E) No error

3. (A) She's looking (B) for a suitcase that (C) can fit all of her clothes, shoes, (D) accessory, and makeup. (E) No error

4. (A) Shawn started taking (B) guitar lessons (C) while he wanted to become (D) a better musician. (E) No error

5. (A) Considering the (B) recent rains we have had, (C) it's a wonder the plants (D) haven't drowned. (E) No error

6. (A) Since none of the furniture (B) were delivered on time (C), we have to move in (D) at a later date. (E) No error

7. It (A) is necessary for instructors (B) to offer tutoring to (C) any students who need (D) extra help in the class. (E) No error

8. The (A) fact the train set only (B) includes four cars and (C) one small track was a big (D) disappointment to my son. (E) No error

9. (A) Because many people (B) feel there are too (C) many distractions to get any work (D) done, I actually enjoy working from home. (E) No error

10. There (A) were many questions about (B) why the case went cold, but the detective (C) wasn't willing to (D) discuss the case with reporters. (E) No error

Revision Skills

For the revision skills section, choose the answer choice that is the best option for the sentence in the passage. If you think the sentence should stay the same, choose Choice A.

Read the selection about traveling in an RV and answer Questions 11–17.

> I have to admit that when my father bought a recreational vehicle (RV), I thought he was making a huge mistake. I didn't really know anything about RVs, but I knew that my dad was as big a "city slicker" as there was. (1) In fact, I even thought he might have gone a little bit crazy. On trips to the beach, he preferred to swim at the pool, and whenever he went hiking, he avoided touching any plants for fear that they might be poison ivy. Why would this man, with an almost irrational fear of the outdoors, want a 40-foot camping behemoth?
>
> (2) The RV was a great purchase for our family and brought us all closer together. Every morning (3) we would wake up, eat breakfast, and broke camp. We laughed at our own comical attempts to back The Beast into spaces that seemed impossibly small. (4) We rejoiced as "hackers." When things inevitably went wrong and we couldn't solve the problems on our own, we discovered the incredible helpfulness and friendliness of the RV community. (5) We even made some new friends in the process.
>
> (6) Above all, it allowed us to share adventures. While traveling across America, which we could not have experienced in cars and hotels. Enjoying a campfire on a chilly summer evening with the mountains of Glacier National Park in the background, or waking up early in the morning to see the sun rising over the distant spires of Arches National Park are memories that will always stay with me and our entire family. (7) Those are also memories that my siblings and me have now shared with our own children.

11. Which of the following would be the best choice for this sentence (reproduced below)?

In fact, I even thought he might have gone a little bit crazy.

a. Keep the sentence as it is.
b. Move the sentence so that it comes before the preceding sentence.
c. Move the sentence to the end of the first paragraph.
d. Omit the sentence.
e. Move this sentence to the beginning of the first paragraph.

12. In context, which is the best version of the underlined portion of this sentence (reproduced below)?

The RV was a great purchase for our family and brought us all closer together.

a. The RV
b. Not surprisingly, the RV
c. Furthermore, the RV
d. As it turns out, the RV
e. Unfortunately, the RV

13. Which is the best version of the underlined portion of this sentence (reproduced below)?

Every morning we would wake up, eat breakfast, and broke camp.

a. we would wake up, eat breakfast, and broke camp.
b. we would woke up, eat breakfast, and broke camp.
c. would we wake up, eat breakfast, and break camp?
d. we are waking up, eating breakfast, and breaking camp.
e. we would wake up, eat breakfast, and break camp.

14. Which is the best version of the underlined portion of this sentence (reproduced below)?

We rejoiced as "hackers."

a. We rejoiced as "hackers."
b. To a nagging problem of technology, we rejoiced as "hackers."
c. We rejoiced when we figured out how to "hack" a solution to a nagging technological problem.
d. To "hack" our way to a solution, we had to rejoice.
e. Although we were hackers, we could still rejoice because of technology.

15. Which is the best version of the underlined portion of this sentence (reproduced below)?

We even made some new friends in the process.

a. We even made some new friends in the process.
b. In the process was the friends we were making.
c. We are even making some new friends in the process.
d. We will make new friends in the process.
e. Making new friends in the process.

16. Which is the best version of the underlined portion of this sentence (reproduced below)?

Above all, it allowed us to share adventures. While traveling across America, which we could not have experienced in cars and hotels.

a. Above all, it allowed us to share adventures. While traveling across America
b. Above all, it allowed us to share adventures while traveling across America
c. Above all, it allowed us to share adventures; while traveling across America
d. Above all, it allowed us to share adventures—while traveling across America
e. Above all it allowed us to share adventures while traveling across America

17. Which is the best version of the underlined portion of this sentence (reproduced below)?

Those are also memories that my siblings and me have now shared with our own children.

a. Those are also memories that my siblings and me
b. Those are also memories that me and my siblings
c. Those are also memories that my siblings and I
d. Those are also memories that I and my siblings
e. Those are also memories that us siblings and I

Read the following section about Fred Hampton and answer Questions 18–28.

Fred Hampton desired to see lasting social change for African American people through nonviolent means and community recognition. (8) In the meantime, he became an African American activist during the American Civil Rights Movement and led the Chicago chapter of the Black Panther Party.

Hampton's Education

Hampton was born and raised (9) in Maywood of Chicago, Illinois in 1948. (10) Gifted academically and a natural athlete, he became a stellar baseball player in high school. After graduating from Proviso East High School in 1966, he later went on to study law at Triton Junior College. While studying at Triton, Hampton joined and became a leader of the National Association for the Advancement of Colored People (NAACP). As a result of his leadership, the NAACP gained more than 500 members. Hampton worked relentlessly to acquire recreational facilities in the neighborhood and improve the educational resources provided to the impoverished black community of Maywood.

The Black Panthers

The Black Panther Party (BPP) (11) was another that formed around the same time as and was similar in function to the NAACP. Hampton was quickly attracted to the (12) Black Panther Party's approach to the fight for equal rights for African Americans. Hampton eventually joined the chapter and relocated to downtown Chicago to be closer to its headquarters.

His charismatic personality, organizational abilities, sheer determination, and rhetorical skills (13) enable him to quickly rise through the chapter's ranks. Hampton soon became the leader of the Chicago chapter of the BPP where he organized rallies, taught political education classes, and established a free medical clinic. (14) He also took part in the community police supervision project. He played an instrumental role in the BPP breakfast program for impoverished African American children.

Hampton's (15) greatest acheivement as the leader of the BPP may be his fight against street gang violence in Chicago. In 1969, (16) Hampton was held by a press conference where he made the gangs agree to a nonaggression pact known as the Rainbow Coalition. As a result of the pact, a multiracial alliance between blacks, Puerto Ricans, and poor youth was developed.

Assassination

(17) As the Black Panther Party's popularity and influence grew, the Federal Bureau of Investigation (FBI) placed the group under constant surveillance. In an attempt to neutralize the party, the FBI launched several harassment campaigns against the BPP, raided its headquarters in Chicago three times, and arrested over one hundred of the group's members. Hampton was shot during such a raid that occurred on the morning of December 4th, 1969.

(18) In 1976; seven years after the event, it was revealed that William O'Neal, Hampton's trusted bodyguard, was an undercover FBI agent. (19) O'Neal will provide the FBI with detailed floor plans of the BPP's headquarters, identifying the exact location of Hampton's bed. It was because of these floor plans that the police were able to target and kill Hampton.

The assassination of Hampton fueled outrage amongst the African American community. It was not until years after the assassination that the police admitted wrongdoing. (20) The Chicago City Council now are commemorating December 4th as Fred Hampton Day.

18. In context, which is the best version of the underlined portion of this sentence (reproduced below)?

In the meantime, he became an African American activist during the American Civil Rights Movement and led the Chicago chapter of the Black Panther Party.

a. In the meantime,
b. Unfortunately,
c. Finally,
d. As a result,
e. Surprisingly,

19. Which is the best version of the underlined portion of this sentence (reproduced below)?

Hampton was born and raised in Maywood of Chicago, Illinois in 1948.

a. in Maywood of Chicago, Illinois in 1948.
b. in Maywood, of Chicago, Illinois in 1948.
c. in Maywood of Chicago, Illinois, in 1948.
d. in Chicago, Illinois of Maywood in 1948.
e. In Maywood Chicago Illinois in 1948.

20. Which of the following sentences, if any, should begin a new paragraph?

Gifted academically and a natural athlete, he became a stellar baseball player in high school. After graduating from Proviso East High School in 1966, he later went on to study law at Triton Junior College. While studying at Triton, Hampton joined and became a leader of the National Association for the Advancement of Colored People (NAACP). As a result of his leadership, the NAACP gained more than 500 members.

a. No change; best as written.
b. Gifted academically and a natural athlete, he became a stellar baseball player in high school.
c. After graduating from Proviso East High School in 1966, he later went on to study law at Triton Junior College.
d. While studying at Triton, Hampton joined and became a leader of the National Association for the Advancement of Colored People (NAACP).
e. As a result of his leadership, the NAACP gained more than 500 members.

21. Which of the following facts would be the most relevant to include here?

The Black Panther Party (BPP) was another that formed around the same time as and was similar in function to the NAACP.

a. was another that
b. had lots of groups that
c. had a lot of members that
d. was another school that
e. was another activist group that

22. Which is the best version of the underlined portion of this sentence (reproduced below)?

Hampton was quickly attracted to the Black Panther Party's approach to the fight for equal rights for African Americans.

a. Black Panther Party's approach
b. Black Panther Parties approach
c. Black Panther Partys' approach
d. Black Panther Parties' approach
e. Black Panther Partys approach

23. Which is the best version of the underlined portion of this sentence (reproduced below)?

His charismatic personality, organizational abilities, sheer determination, and rhetorical skills enable him to quickly rise through the chapter's ranks.

a. enable him to quickly rise
b. are enabling him to quickly rise
c. enabled him to quickly rise
d. will enable him to quickly rise
e. can enable him to quickly rise

24. Which is the best version of the underlined portion of this sentence (reproduced below)?

He also took part in the community police supervision project. He played an instrumental role in the BPP breakfast program for impoverished African American children.

a. He also took part in the community police supervision project. He played an instrumental role
b. He also took part in the community police supervision project but played an instrumental role
c. He also took part in the community police supervision project, he played an instrumental role
d. He also took part in the community police supervision project and played an instrumental role
e. He also took part in the community police supervision project; and played an instrumental role

25. Which of these, if any, is misspelled?

Hampton's (15) greatest acheivement as the leader of the BPP may be his fight against street gang violence in Chicago.

a. (No change; best as written.)
b. greatest
c. acheivement
d. leader
e. against

26. Which is the best version of the underlined portion of this sentence (reproduced below)?

In 1969, Hampton was held by a press conference where he made the gangs agree to a nonaggression pact known as the Rainbow Coalition.

a. Hampton was held by a press conference
b. Hampton held a press conference
c. Hampton, holding a press conference
d. Hampton to hold a press conference
e. Hampton was held a press conference

27. Which is the best version of the underlined portion of this sentence (reproduced below)?

As the Black Panther Party's popularity and influence grew, the Federal Bureau of Investigation (FBI) placed the group under constant surveillance.

a. As the Black Panther Party's popularity and influence grew, the Federal Bureau of Investigation (FBI) placed the group under constant surveillance.
b. The Federal Bureau of Investigation (FBI) placed the group under constant surveillance as the Black Panther Party's popularity and influence grew.
c. Placing the group under constant surveillance, the Black Panther Party's popularity and influence grew.
d. As their influence and popularity grew, the FBI placed the group under constant surveillance.
e. Under constant surveillance the Black Panther Party's popularity and influence grew thanks to the FBI.

28. Which is the best version of the underlined portion of this sentence (reproduced below)?

In 1976; seven years after the event, it was revealed that William O'Neal, Hampton's trusted bodyguard, was an undercover FBI agent.

a. In 1976; seven years after the event,
b. In 1976, seven years after the event,
c. In 1976 seven years after the event,
d. In 1976. Seven years after the event,
e. In 1976; seven years after the event;

Ability to Use Source Materials

The following questions test research, reference, and writing skills. Some refer to passages while the others are self-contained.

29. **peak** *n*. 1. The sharp or pointed top of a mountain 2. A mountain with a sharp or pointed summit 3. The highest or most important level of something, such as a career | Synonyms: pinnacle, acme, zenith | [From Old English *Peaclond*, from the district of *Pecsaetan*]

Which of the following statements is NOT supported by the definition above?
a. The word "peak" denotes reaching the highest point of something.
b. "Acme" can be a synonym for the word "peak."
c. The definitions above represent the word "peak" as it is in noun form.
d. The word "peak" is from the Old English "Peaclond."
e. The word "peak" is always used to refer to mountains.

30. Guerin, Wilfred L., et al. *A Handbook of Critical Approaches to Literature*. Oxford University Press, 2011.

In the above citation, the abbreviation "et al." indicates that the book
a. has an author who is deceased.
b. has more than one author.
c. has more than one publication date.
d. was published before the presented date.
e. is both a book and a journal.

31. Shannon, M., Bohn, P., Elimelech, M., Georgiadis, J., Marinas, B. and Mayes, A. (2008). Science and technology for water purification in the coming decades. *Nature*, 452(7185), pp. 301-310.

In the above citation, what information is provided by the number "452"?
a. The volume number
b. The issue number
c. The abbreviated date
d. The page number
e. The year

32. *The following excerpt is taken from a student's research paper in MLA format.*

> Fred Bowers, digging through the Valentine Collection where they keep the majority of the manuscripts for Whitman's 1860 edition of *Leaves of Grass*, discovered that Whitman's original spark of "Calamus," sent to the Rome Brothers in 1959, was a cluster of twelve poems from the "Calamus" group called "Live Oak, with Moss" (Bowers 259).

What does the phrase in the parenthesis indicate?
- a. Title, page number
- b. Author, page number
- c. Author, volume
- d. Title, volume
- e. Journal, issue number

33. Arora, Isha. "Indian Manufacturing PMI Growth Slows in May, Inflationary..." Bloomberg, Thomson Reuters, 1 June 2018, in.reuters.com/article/india-economy-pmi/indian-manufacturing-pmi-growth-slows-in-may-inflationary-pressures-pick-up-idINKCN1IX3MJ.

In the citation shown above, what information is provided by the date "1 June 2018"?
- a. The date the article was written.
- b. The date the website was accessed.
- c. The date the article was electronically published.
- d. The date the website was published.
- e. The date the article was uploaded onto the website.

Questions 34–41 are based on the following passage:

> (1) Naturally, the poem's popularity can be attributed both to Wakefield's performance and the quality of his writing. (2) "Crowbirds" touches on themes of core human concepts such as faith, personal loss, and growth. (3) These are not ideas that only poets or students of literature understand, but all human beings: "You acted like I was hurling crowbirds at mockingbars / and abandoned me for not making sense. / Evidently, I don't experience things as rationally as you do" (Wakefield 15-17). (4) Wakefield weaves together a complex description of the perplexed and hurt emotions of the speaker undergoing a separation from a romantic interest. (5) The line "You acted like I was hurling crowbirds at mockingbars" conjures up an image of someone confused, seemingly out of their mind . . . or in the case of the speaker, passionately trying to grasp at a relationship that is fading. (6) The speaker is looking back and finding the words that described how he wasn't making sense. (7) This poem is particularly human and gripping in its message but the entire effect of the poem is enhanced through the physical performance.
>
> (8) Although the platform may look different, poetry continues to have a steady audience due to the emotional connection the poet shares with the audience. (9) At its core, poetry is about addressing issues/ideas in the world. (10) Part of this is also addressing the perspectives that are exiguously considered.

34. What type of in-text citation is represented in sentence 3?
   a. A newspaper
   b. A poem
   c. A website
   d. A magazine
   e. A book

35. The information in parenthesis at the end of sentence 3 informs the reader that
   a. The name of the quoted material is "Wakefield" and it's on the page numbers 15–17.
   b. The quoted material is written by Wakefield and the page numbers are 15–17.
   c. The title of the article quoted is "Wakefield" and it's in the issues 15–17.
   d. The quoted material is in a book called *Wakefield* and it's volume numbers are 15–17.
   e. The quoted material is written by Wakefield and the lines represented are 15–17.

36. The author of the passage uses the quote in line 5 to
   a. convince the audience that the speaker is unhinged.
   b. instigate an argument revolving around the characters.
   c. persuade the audience that the poem lacks substance.
   d. analyze the significance of that line in the poem.
   e. relay the message of love in the eyes of the speaker.

37. The author of the passage would likely agree most with which of the following?
   a. Buddy Wakefield is a genius and is considered at the forefront of modern poetry.
   b. Poetry is not irrelevant; it is an art form that adapts to the changing time while containing its core elements.
   c. Spoken word is the zenith of poetic forms and the premier style of poetry in this decade.
   d. Poetry is on the verge of vanishing from our cultural consciousness.
   e. Poetry is irrelevant to modern society and we should therefore focus on film instead.

38. Which one of the following words, if substituted for the word *exiguously* in the last paragraph, would LEAST change the meaning of the sentence?
   a. Indolently
   b. Inaudibly
   c. Interminably
   d. Infrequently
   e. Indelibly

39. In sentence 2, why is the word "Crowbirds" in quotes?
   a. It's the title of a play.
   b. It's the title of a journal.
   c. It's the title of a film.
   d. It's the title of a novel.
   e. It's the title of a poem.

40. Which of the following is missing in sentence 7?
    a. A comma after the word "human."
    b. The word "effect" should be "affect."
    c. A comma after the word "message."
    d. The word "physical" should be spelled "phisycal."
    e. "is enhanced" should be "enhances."

41. Which is best to do with sentence 8 (reproduced below)?

> Although the platform may look different, poetry continues to have a steady audience due to the emotional connection the poet shares with the audience.

    a. Keep where it is now.
    b. Move to the end of the first paragraph.
    c. Move to the end of the paragraph as the concluding sentence.
    d. Make the sentence its own paragraph.
    e. Place between sentence 9 and sentence 10.

Questions 42–46 are based upon the following passage:

This excerpt is adapted from *Our Vanishing Wildlife,* by William T. Hornaday

> Three years ago, I think there were not many bird-lovers in the United States who believed it possible to prevent the total extinction of both egrets from our fauna. All the known rookeries accessible to plume-hunters had been totally destroyed. Two years ago, the secret discovery of several small, hidden colonies prompted William Dutcher, President of the National Association of Audubon Societies, and Mr. T. Gilbert Pearson, Secretary, to attempt the protection of those colonies. With a fund contributed for the purpose, wardens were hired and duly commissioned. As previously stated, one of those wardens was shot dead in cold blood by a plume hunter. The task of guarding swamp rookeries from the attacks of money-hungry desperadoes to whom the accursed plumes were worth their weight in gold, is a very chancy proceeding. There is now one warden in Florida who says that "before they get my rookery they will first have to get me."
>
> Thus far the protective work of the Audubon Association has been successful. Now there are twenty colonies, which contain all told, about 5,000 egrets and about 120,000 herons and ibises which are guarded by the Audubon wardens. One of the most important is on Bird Island, a mile out in Orange Lake, central Florida, and it is ably defended by Oscar E. Baynard. To-day, the plume hunters who do not dare to raid the guarded rookeries are trying to study out the lines of flight of the birds, to and from their feeding-grounds, and shoot them in transit. Their motto is—"Anything to beat the law, and get the plumes." It is there that the state of Florida should take part in the war.
>
> The success of this campaign is attested by the fact that last year a number of egrets were seen in eastern Massachusetts—for the first time in many years. And so to-day the question is, can the wardens continue to hold the plume-hunters at bay?

42. The author's use of first-person pronouns in the following text does NOT have which of the following effects?

> Three years ago, I think there were not many bird-lovers in the United States who believed it possible to prevent the total extinction of both egrets from our fauna.

a. The phrase *I think* acts as a sort of hedging, where the author's tone is less direct and/or absolute.
b. It allows the reader to more easily connect with the author.
c. It encourages the reader to empathize with the egrets.
d. It distances the reader from the text by overemphasizing the story.
e. It enhances the trust between the reader and the author.

43. What purpose does the quote serve at the end of the first paragraph?
a. The quote shows proof of a hunter threatening one of the wardens.
b. The quote lightens the mood by illustrating the colloquial language of the region.
c. The quote provides an example of a warden protecting one of the colonies.
d. The quote provides much needed comic relief in the form of a joke.
e. The quote assures the reader that the rookeries are safe.

44. What is the meaning of the word *rookeries* in the following text?

> To-day, the plume hunters who do not dare to raid the guarded rookeries are trying to study out the lines of flight of the birds, to and from their feeding-grounds, and shoot them in transit.

a. Houses in a slum area
b. A place where hunters gather to trade tools
c. A place where wardens go to trade stories
d. A colony of breeding birds
e. A sort of zoo where animals are kept.

45. What is on Bird Island?
a. Hunters selling plumes
b. An important bird colony
c. Bird Island Battle between the hunters and the wardens
d. An important egret with unique plumes
e. A community of wardens.

46. What is the main purpose of the passage?
a. To persuade the audience to act in preservation of the bird colonies
b. To show the effect hunting egrets has had on the environment
c. To argue that the preservation of bird colonies has had a negative impact on the environment
d. To demonstrate the success of the protective work of the Audubon Association
e. To inform readers of the history of violence between hunters and wardens

Rhetorical Analysis

The questions below test your skills in analyzing writing. Some questions refer to the passages while some are self-contained.

Questions 47–49 are based on the following passage:

> The town of Alexandria, Virginia was founded in 1749. Between the years 1810 and 1861, this thriving seaport was the ideal location for slave owners such as Joseph Bruin, Henry Hill, Isaac Franklin, and John Armfield to build several slave trade office structures, including slave holding areas. After 1830, when the manufacturing-based economy slowed down in Virginia, slaves were traded to plantations in the Deep South, in Alabama, Mississippi, and Louisiana. Joseph Bruin, one of the most notorious of the slave traders operating in Alexandria, alone purchased hundreds of slaves from 1844 to 1861. Harriet Beecher Stowe claimed that the horrible slave traders mentioned in her novel, *Uncle Tom's Cabin*, are reminiscent of the coldhearted Joseph Bruin. The Franklin and Armfield Office was known as one of the largest slave trading companies in the country up to the end of the Civil War period. Slaves, waiting to be traded, were held in a two-story slave pen built behind the Franklin and Armfield Office structure on Duke Street in Alexandria. Yet, many people fought to thwart these traders and did everything they could to rescue and free slaves. Two Christian African American slave sisters, with the help of northern abolitionists who bought their freedom, escaped Bruin's plan to sell them into southern prostitution. In 1861, Joseph Bruin was captured and imprisoned and his property confiscated. The Bruin Slave Jail became the Fairfax County courthouse until 1865. The original Franklin and Armfield Office building still stands in Virginia and is registered in the National Register of Historic Places. The Bruin Slave Jail is still standing on Duke Street in Alexandria, but is not open to the public. The history of the slave trading enterprise is preserved and presented to the public by the Northern Virginia Urban League.

47. Based on the above passage, which of the following statements about the town of Alexandria are true?

a. Alexandria was a seaport town, which could not prosper, even with the advent of a slave trade business, because the manufacturing industry was not enough to stabilize the economy.
b. Slave traders such as Joseph Bruin, Henry Hill, Isaac Franklin, and John Armfield rented both slave trade office buildings and slave holding buildings from landlords of Old Town, Alexandria.
c. For over fifteen years, Joseph Bruin, a notorious slave trader, probably the one characterized in *Uncle Tom's Cabin*, bought hundreds of slaves with the intention of sending the purchased slaves to southern states such as Alabama, Mississippi, and Louisiana.
d. The Bruin Slave Jail is open to the public; the building is located in downtown Alexandria, and still stands in Virginia. The jail is registered in the National Register of Historic Places. The history of the slave trading enterprise is preserved and presented to the public by the Northern Virginia Urban League.
e. Isaac Franklin and John Armfield's slave-trade office structures, including slave holding areas in downtown Alexandria, did not remain open for their slave trade business until the end of the Civil War.

48. The passage about the Alexandria slave trade business suggests that which of the following statements can be regarded as true?

a. The lucrative seaport town of Alexandria was supported by successful slave trade businesses of men like Joseph Bruin, Henry Hill, Isaac Franklin, and John Armfield, who bought slaves and sold them to the plantations in the Deep South.
b. Joseph Bruin, a highly respected Alexandrian businessman, ran a slave trade business in downtown Alexandria, until the business closed its doors at the end of the Civil War.
c. The Franklin and Armfield Office was built by Isaac Franklin and John Armfield. Slaves, waiting to be traded, were held in a four-story slave pen built behind the Franklin and Armfield Office structure on Duke Street in Alexandria.
d. When the Confederate Army positioned its command in Alexandria, and closed slave traders' businesses, the Franklin and Armfield slave pen became the Fairfax County courthouse and was used to hold Union soldiers.
e. The literature of the slave trading enterprise, like *Uncle Tom's Cabin*, is being preserved and presented to the public by the Northern Virginia Urban League.

49. Which of the following statements best illustrates the author's intended main point or thesis?

a. Two Christian African American slave sisters, with the help of northern abolitionists who bought their freedom, escaped Bruin's plan to sell them into southern prostitution.
b. The town of Alexandria, a thriving seaport founded in 1749, was the location for several lucrative slave trading companies from 1810 to 1861.
c. After the start of the Civil War, Joseph Bruin was captured and his jail was no longer used for his slave trade business.
d. The Bruin Slave Jail is still standing on Duke Street in Alexandria, but is not open to the public.
e. In 1861, the Bruin Slave Jail in Alexandria became the Fairfax County courthouse.

Questions 50–53 are based on the following passage:

Becoming a successful leader in today's industry, government, and nonprofit sectors requires more than a high intelligence quotient (IQ). Emotional Intelligence (EI) includes developing the ability to know one's own emotions, to regulate impulses and emotions, and to use interpersonal communication skills with ease while dealing with other people. A combination of knowledge, skills, abilities, and mature emotional intelligence (EI) reflects the most effective leadership recipe. Successful leaders sharpen more than their talents and IQ levels; they practice the basic features of emotional intelligence. Some of the hallmark traits of a competent, emotionally intelligent leader include self-efficacy, drive, determination, collaboration, vision, humility, and openness to change. An unsuccessful leader exhibits opposite leadership traits: unclear directives, inconsistent vision and planning strategies, disrespect for followers, incompetence, and an uncompromising transactional leadership style. There are ways to develop emotional intelligence for the person who wants to improve his or her leadership style. For example, an emotionally intelligent leader creates an affirmative environment by incorporating collaborative activities, using professional development training for employee self-awareness, communicating clearly about the organization's vision, and developing a variety of resources for working with emotions. Building relationships outside the institution with leadership coaches and with professional development trainers can also help leaders who want to grow their leadership success. Leaders in today's work environment need to strive for a combination of skill, knowledge, and mature emotional intelligence to lead followers to success and to promote the vision and mission of their respective institutions.

50. The passage suggests that the term *emotional intelligence (EI)* can be defined as which of the following?

a. A combination of knowledge, skills, abilities, and mature emotional intelligence reflects the most effective EI leadership recipe.
b. An emotionally intelligent leader creates an affirmative environment by incorporating collaborative activities, using professional development training for employee self-awareness, communicating clearly about the organization's vision, and developing a variety of resources for working with emotions.
c. EI includes developing the ability to know one's own emotions, to regulate impulses and emotions, and to use interpersonal communication skills with ease while dealing with other people.
d. Becoming a successful leader in today's industry, government, and nonprofit sectors requires more than a high IQ.
e. An EI leader exhibits the following leadership traits: unclear directives, inconsistent vision and planning strategies, disrespect for followers, incompetence, and uncompromising transactional leadership style.

51. Based on the information in the passage, a successful leader must have a high EI quotient.

a. The above statement can be supported by the fact that Daniel Goldman conducted a scientific study.
b. The above statement can be supported by the example that emotionally intelligent people are highly successful leaders.
c. The above statement is not supported by the passage.
d. The above statement is supported by the illustration that claims, "Leaders in today's work environment need to strive for a combination of skill, knowledge, and mature emotional intelligence to lead followers to success and to promote the vision and mission of their respective institutions."
e. The above statement can be inferred because emotionally intelligent people obviously make successful leaders.

52. According to the passage above, some of the characteristics of an unsuccessful leader include which of the following?

a. Talent, IQ level, and abilities
b. Humility, knowledge, and skills
c. Loud, demeaning actions toward female employees
d. Outdated technological resources and strategies
e. Transactional leadership style

53. According to the passage above, which of the following must be true?

a. The leader exhibits a healthy work/life balance lifestyle.
b. The leader is uncompromising in transactional directives for all employees, regardless of status.
c. The leader learns to strategize using future trends analysis to create a five-year plan.
d. The leader uses a combination of skill, knowledge, and mature reasoning to make decisions.
e. The leader continually tries to improve his or her EI test quotient by studying the intelligence quotient of other successful leaders.

Questions 54–57 are based on the following passage:

Learning how to write a ten-minute play may seem like a monumental task at first; but, if you follow a simple creative writing strategy, similar to writing a narrative story, you will be able to write a successful drama. The first step is to open your story as if it is a puzzle to be solved. This will allow the reader a moment to engage with the story and to mentally solve the story with you, the author. Immediately provide descriptive details that steer the main idea, the tone, and the mood according to the overarching theme you have in mind. For example, if the play is about something ominous, you may open Scene One with a thunderclap. Next, use dialogue to reveal the attitudes and personalities of each of the characters who have a key part in the unfolding story. Keep the characters off balance in some way to create interest and dramatic effect. Maybe what the characters say does not match what they do. Show images on stage to speed up the narrative; remember, one picture speaks a thousand words. As the play progresses, the protagonist must cross the point of no return in some way; this is the climax of the story. Then, as in a written story, you create a resolution to the life-changing event of the protagonist. Let the characters experience some kind of self-discovery that can be understood and appreciated by the patient audience. Finally, make sure all things come together in the end so that every detail in the play makes sense right before the curtain falls.

54. Based on the passage above, which of the following statements is FALSE?
    a. Writing a ten-minute play may seem like an insurmountable task.
    b. Providing descriptive details is not necessary until after the climax of the story line.
    c. Engaging the audience by jumping into the story line immediately helps the audience solve the story's developing ideas with you, the writer.
    d. Descriptive details give clues to the play's intended mood and tone.
    e. The introduction of a ten-minute play does not need to open with a lot of coffee pouring or cigarette smoking to introduce the scenes. The action can get started right away.

55. In the passage above, the writer suggests that writing a ten-minute play is accessible for a novice playwright because of which of the following reasons?
    a. It took the author of the passage only one week to write his first play.
    b. The format follows similar strategies of writing a narrative story.
    c. There are no particular themes or points to unravel; a playwright can use a stream of consciousness style to write a play.
    d. Dialogue that reveals the characters' particularities is uncommonly simple to write.
    e. The characters of a ten-minute play wrap up the action simply by revealing their ideas in a monologue.

56. Based on the passage above, which basic feature of narrative writing is NOT mentioned with respect to writing a ten-minute play?
    a. Character development
    b. Descriptive details
    c. Dialogue
    d. Mood and tone
    e. Style

57. Based on the passage above, which of the following is true?
   a. The class of eighth graders quickly learned that it is not that difficult to write a ten-minute play.
   b. The playwrights of the twenty-first century all use the narrative writing basic feature guide to outline their initial scripts.
   c. In order to follow a simple structure, a person can write a ten-minute play based on some narrative writing features.
   d. Women find playwriting easier than men because they are used to communicating in writing.
   e. The structure of writing a poem is similar to that of play writing and of narrative writing.

Improving Sentences

Choose the option that corrects an error in the underlined portion. If no error exists, choose Choice A.

58. Early in my career, a master's teacher shared this thought with me "Education is the last bastion of civility."

   a. a master's teacher shared this thought with me "Education is the last bastion of civility."
   b. a master's teacher shared this thought with me: "Education is the last bastion of civility."
   c. a master's teacher shared this thought with me: "Education is the last bastion of civility".
   d. a master's teacher shared this thought with me. "Education is the last bastion of civility."
   e. a master' teacher shared this thought with me; "Education is the last bastion of civility."

59. Which of the following words is spelled incorrectly?

   It is really what makes us human and what distinguishes us as civilised creatures.

   a. makes
   b. human
   c. distinguishes
   d. civilised
   e. creatures

60. Education should never discriminate on any basis, and it should create individuals who are self-sufficient, patriotic, and tolerant of others' ideas.

   a. others' ideas
   b. other's ideas
   c. others ideas
   d. others's ideas
   e. "others" ideas

61. All children can learn. Although not all children learn in the same manner.

   a. All children can learn. Although not all children learn in the same manner.
   b. All children can learn although not all children learn in the same manner.
   c. All children can learn although, not all children learn in the same manner.
   d. All children can learn, although not all children learn in the same manner.
   e. All children can learn . . . although . . . not all children learn in the same manner.

62. If teachers set high expectations for there students, the students will rise to that high level.

a. there students
b. they're students
c. their students
d. his students
e. her students

63. In the modern age of technology, a teacher's focus is no longer the "what" of the content, but more importantly, the 'why.'

a. but more importantly, the 'why.'
b. but more importantly, the "why."
c. but more importantly, the 'why'.
d. but more importantly, the "why".
e. but more importantly the why.

64. Students have to read between the lines, identify bias, and determine who they can trust in the milieu of ads, data, and texts presented to them.

a. read between the lines, identify bias, and determine
b. read between the lines, identify bias, and determining
c. read between the lines, identifying bias, and determining
d. reads between the lines, identifies bias, and determines
e. reading between the lines, identify bias, and determine

65. During their time in present-day Newfoundland, Leif's expedition made contact with the natives whom they referred to as Skraelings (which translates to 'wretched ones' in Norse).

a. (which translates to 'wretched ones' in Norse).
b. (which translates to "wretched ones" in Norse.)
c. (which translates to 'wretched ones' in Norse.)
d. (which translates to "wretched ones" in Norse).
e. which translates to (wretched ones) in Norse.

Answer Explanations

Conventions of Standard Written English

1. A: Choice *A* is correct because the article (*an*) and the noun (*issues*) do not agree in number. It should be written as "Important issues" or "An important issue."

2. B: Choice *B* is correct because it uses an -ing verb "attributing," which is an incorrect verb choice. The verb phrase most appropriate here should be "can be attributed."

3. D: Choice *D* is correct because it uses incorrect parallel structure of plural nouns. The word "accessory" should be "accessories" so to fit with the rest of the plural nouns.

4. C: In a cause/effect relationship, it is correct to use the word because in the clausal part of the sentence. Choice *C* uses "while," but the word "because" fits better here because it's showing a cause and effect relationship.

5. E: There is no error in this sentence.

6. B: Choice *B* contains an error because of the subject/verb agreement. The sentence should read "none of the furniture was delivered on time," not "were delivered." The subject to pay attention to here is "none," so we would say "none . . . was," a singular subject and a singular verb.

7. E: There is no error in this sentence.

8. A: Choice *A* is missing the word *that*, which is necessary for the sentence to make sense. This is the only answer choice with an error.

9. A: The word "Because" is incorrect here because the sentence is not stating cause and effect. The word "While" would work much better here because it indicates a contrast.

10. E: There is no error in this sentence.

Revision Skills

11. B: Move the sentence so that it comes before the preceding sentence. For this question, place the underlined sentence in each prospective choice's position. To keep it as-is is incorrect because the father "going crazy" doesn't logically follow the fact that he was a "city slicker." Choice *C* is incorrect because the sentence in question is not a concluding sentence and does not transition smoothly into the second paragraph. Choice *D* is incorrect because the sentence doesn't necessarily need to be omitted since it logically follows the very first sentence in the passage. Choice *E* is incorrect; this would not work as an appropriate introductory sentence.

12. D: Choice *D* is correct because "As it turns out" indicates a contrast from the previous sentiment, that the RV was a great purchase. Choice *A* is incorrect because the sentence needs an effective transition from the paragraph before. Choice *B* is incorrect because the text indicates it *is* surprising that the RV was a great purchase because the author was skeptical beforehand. Choice *C* is incorrect because the transition "Furthermore" does not indicate a contrast. Choice *E* is incorrect; the tone of the passage indicates it would not be unfortunate for the family to be brought closer together.

13. E: This sentence calls for parallel structure. Choice *E* is correct because the verbs "wake," "eat," and "break" are consistent in tense and parts of speech. Choice *A* is incorrect because the words "wake" and "eat" are present tense while the word "broke" is in past tense. Choice *B* is incorrect because "would woke" is not a grammatically correct verb phrase to use. Choice *C* is incorrect because this turns the sentence into a question, which doesn't make sense within the context. Choice *D* is incorrect because it breaks tense with the rest of the passage. "Waking," "eating," and "breaking" are all present participles, and the context around the sentence is in past tense.

14. C: Choice *C* is correct because it provides clarity and fits within the context of the passage. Choice *A* is incorrect because "We rejoiced as 'hackers'" does not give a reason why hacking was rejoiced. Choice *B* is incorrect because it does not mention a solution being found and is therefore not specific enough. Choice *D* is incorrect because the meaning is eschewed by the helping verb "had to rejoice," and the sentence suggests that rejoicing was necessary to "hack" a solution. Choice *E* is incorrect because the phrase "because of technology" does not give enough detail to explain why they rejoiced.

15. A: The original sentence is correct because the verb tense, as well as the meaning, aligns with the rest of the passage. Choice *B* is incorrect because the order of the words makes the sentence more confusing than it otherwise would be. Choice *C* is incorrect because "We are even making" is in present tense. Choice *D* is incorrect because "We will make" is future tense. The surrounding text of the sentence is in past tense. Choice *E* is incorrect because there is no subject.

16. B: Choice *B* is correct because there is no punctuation needed if a dependent clause ("while traveling across America") is located behind the independent clause ("it allowed us to share adventures"). Choice *A* is incorrect because there are two dependent clauses connected and no independent clause, and a complete sentence requires at least one independent clause. Choice *C* is incorrect because of the same reason as Choice *A*. Semicolons have the same function as periods: there must be an independent clause on either side of the semicolon. Choice *D* is incorrect because the dash simply interrupts the complete sentence. Choice *E* is incorrect because there is no comma after the introductory phrase "Above all."

17. C: The rules for "me" and "I" is that one should use "I" when it is the subject pronoun of a sentence, and "me" when it is the object pronoun of the sentence. Break the sentence up to see if "I" or "me" should be used. To say "Those are memories that I have now shared" is correct, rather than "Those are memories that me have now shared." Choice *D* is incorrect because "my siblings" should come before "I." Choice *E* is incorrect because the pronoun "us" should be "my."

18. D: Choice *D* is correct because Fred Hampton becoming an activist was a direct result of him wanting to see lasting social change for black people. Choice *A* doesn't make sense because "In the meantime" denotes something happening at the same time as another thing. Choice *B* is incorrect because the text's tone does not indicate that becoming a civil rights activist is an unfortunate path. Choice *C* is incorrect because "Finally" indicates something that comes last in a series of events, and the word in question is at the beginning of the introductory paragraph. Choice *E* is incorrect; it is not surprising he became an activist in this context.

19. A: Choice *A* is correct because there should be a comma between the city and state. Choice *B* is incorrect because the comma after "Maywood" interrupts the phrase "Maywood of Chicago." Choice *C* is incorrect because a comma after "Illinois" is unnecessary. Choice *D* is incorrect because the order of the sentence designates that Chicago, Illinois is in Maywood, which is incorrect. Choice *E* is incorrect because it contains no punctuation.

20. D: This is a difficult question. The paragraph is incorrect as-is because it is too long and thus loses the reader halfway through. Choice *D* is correct because if the new paragraph began with "While studying at Triton," we would see a smooth transition from one paragraph to the next. We can also see how the two paragraphs are logically split in two. The first half of the paragraph talks about where he studied. The second half of the paragraph talks about the NAACP and the result of his leadership in the association. If we look at the passage as a whole, we can see that there are two main topics that should be broken into two separate paragraphs.

21. E: The BPP is another activist group. We can figure out this answer by looking at context clues. We know that the BPP is "similar in function" to the NAACP. To find out what the NAACP's function is, we must look at the previous sentences. We know from above that the NAACP is an activist group, so we can assume that the BPP is also an activist group.

22. A: Choice *A* is correct because the Black Panther Party is one entity; therefore, the possession should show the "Party's approach" with the apostrophe between the "y" and the "s." Choice *B* is incorrect because the word "Parties" should not be plural. Choice *C* is incorrect because the apostrophe indicates that the word "Partys" is plural. The plural of "party" is "parties." Choice *D* is incorrect because, again, the word "parties" should not be plural; instead, it is one unified party. Choice *E* is incorrect because "partys" is not a word. The plural of "party" is "parties."

23. C: Choice *C* is correct because the passage is told in past tense, and "enabled" is a past tense verb. Choice *A,* "enable," is present tense. Choice *B*, "are enabling," is a present participle, which suggests a continuing action. Choice *D*, "will enable," is future tense. Choice *E* "can enable," is incorrect here because the helping verb "can" expresses opportunity and not a past action that has already happened.

24. D: Choice *D* is correct because the conjunction "and" is the best way to combine the two independent clauses. Choice *A* is incorrect because the word "he" becomes repetitive since the two clauses can be joined together. Choice *B* is incorrect because the conjunction "but" indicates a contrast, and there is no contrast between the two clauses. Choice *C* is incorrect because the introduction of the comma after "project" with no conjunction creates a comma splice. Choice *E* is incorrect; a semicolon shouldn't be used to replace a comma. Semicolons are used to separate two independent clauses.

25. C: The word "acheivement" is misspelled. Remember the rules for "*i* before *e* except after *c*." Choices *B* and *D*, "greatest" and "leader," are both spelled correctly, as is Choice *E*, "against."

26. B: Choice *B* is correct because it provides the correct verb tense and verb form. Choice *A* is incorrect; Hampton was not "held by a press conference"—rather, he held a press conference. The passage indicates that he "made the gangs agree to a nonaggression pact," implying that it was Hampton who was doing the speaking for this conference. Choice *C* is incorrect because, with this use of the sentence, it would create a fragment because the verb "holding" has no helping verb in front of it. Choice *D* is incorrect because it adds an infinitive ("to hold") where a past tense form of a verb should be. Choice *E* is incorrect because the helping verb "was" is unnecessary here.

27. A: Choice *A* is correct because it provides the most clarity. Choice *B* is incorrect because it doesn't name the group until the end, so the phrase "the group" is vague. Choice *C* is incorrect because it indicates that the BPP's popularity grew as a result of placing the group under constant surveillance, which is incorrect. Choice *D* is incorrect because there is a misplaced modifier; this sentence actually says that the FBI's influence and popularity grew, which is incorrect. In Choice *E*, it is unclear who placed them under constant surveillance, as "FBI" is mentioned at the end of the sentence.

28. B: Choice *B* is correct. Choice *A* is incorrect because there should be an independent clause on either side of a semicolon, and the phrase "In 1976" is not an independent clause. Choice *C* is incorrect because there should be a comma after introductory phrases in general, such as "In 1976," and Choice *C* omits a comma. Choice *D* is incorrect because the sentence "In 1976." is a fragment. Choice *E* is incorrect; a semicolon is used to separate two independent clauses, and not act as a comma to an introductory phrase.

Ability to Use Source Materials

29. E: Choice *E* is the answer choice that is not supported by the definition. The word "peak" isn't always used to refer to mountains. The third definition refers to the highest level you can reach at something, like a career, so Choice *E* is correct.

30. B: Choice *B* is the best answer choice. The abbreviation "et al." indicates that the book has more than one author. The main author is listed in the citation while the others are left off to keep the citation brief.

31. A: The number "452" in this citation indicates the volume number of the article, Choice *A*. The issue number is the number in parenthesis. The page number is after the letters "pp." The date is in parenthesis as well (2008).

32. B: The phrase in the parenthesis indicates author then page number. In MLA style format, an in-text citation needs an author's last name, if available, followed by the page number, if available.

33. C: This date indicates the date the article was electronically published. Sometimes citations require the date of access: but if they do, there will be a word indicating it, such as *Accessed* 1 June 2018.

34. B: The in-text citation in sentence 3 represents a poem. When a poem is represented in a quote, you'll see the backslash (/) represent the line breaks in poems.

35. E: The quoted material is written by Wakefield and the lines represented are 15–17. When citing a poem, the author's last name should go in parenthesis followed by the line numbers.

36. D: The author is trying to analyze the significance of that line in the poem. They state multiple explanations of what the line could mean, from the speaker being confused to the speaker grasping at a relationship.

37. B: Choice *B* accurately describes the author's argument in the text: that poetry is not irrelevant. This is shown in the last paragraph, or conclusion, of the passage. The last sentence says: "Although the platform may look different, poetry continues to have a steady audience due to the emotional connection the poet shares with the audience."

38. D: *Exiguously* means not occurring often, or occurring rarely, so Choice *D* would LEAST change the meaning of the sentence. Choice *A*, *indolently*, means unhurriedly, or slow, and does not fit the context of the sentence. Choice *B*, *inaudibly*, means quietly or silently. Choice *C*, *interminably*, means endlessly, or all the time, and is the opposite of the word *exiguously*. Choice *E*, indelibly, means making marks that cannot be erased.

39. E: "Crowbirds" is the title of a poem. Plays, journals, films, and novels all use italics for titles. Poems and short stories use quotes for titles.

40. C: There should be a comma after the word "message." The word "message" separates two independent clauses. Independent clauses have a subject and a verb and can stand on their own as sentences. Therefore, they need commas before the conjunction that separates them.

41. C: This sentence should be moved to the end of the paragraph as the concluding sentence. This sentence wraps up a main idea that poetry is still alive in a modern setting. This is the best concluding sentence because it offers a final argument to the reader.

42. D: The use of "I" could serve to have a "hedging" effect, allow the reader to connect with the author in a more personal way, and cause the reader to empathize more with the egrets. However, it doesn't distance the reader from the text, making Choice *D* the answer to this question.

43. C: The quote provides an example of a warden protecting one of the colonies. Choice *A* is incorrect because the speaker of the quote is a warden, not a hunter. Choice B is incorrect because the quote does not lighten the mood but shows the danger of the situation between the wardens and the hunters. Choice *D* is incorrect because there is no humor found in the quote. Choice *E* is incorrect; the rookeries are not safe at this point in the passage.

44. D: A *rookery* is a colony of breeding birds. Although *rookery* could mean Choice *A*, houses in a slum area, it does not make sense in this context. Choices *B* and *C* are both incorrect, as this is not a place for hunters to trade tools or for wardens to trade stories. Choice *E* is also incorrect, as rookeries are not considered a sort of zoo.

45. B: An important bird colony. The previous sentence is describing "twenty colonies" of birds, so what follows should be a bird colony. Choice *A* may be true, but we have no evidence of this in the text. Choice *C* does touch on the tension between the hunters and wardens, but there is no official "Bird Island Battle" mentioned in the text. Choices *D* and *E* do not exist in the text.

46. D: To demonstrate the success of the protective work of the Audubon Association. The text mentions several different times how and why the association has been successful and gives examples to back this fact. Choice *A* is incorrect because although the article, in some instances, calls certain people to act, it is not the purpose of the entire passage. There is no way to tell if Choices *B* and *C* are correct, as they are not mentioned in the text. Choice *E* is incorrect; there is violence between wardens and hunters but we are not told the full history of it.

Rhetorical Analysis

47. C: Choice *A* is incorrect because the seaport is noted as "thriving"; also, the slave trading companies were noted as being "lucrative." Choice *B* is incorrect because the slave traders actually built both office structures and slave holding buildings in downtown Alexandria; there is no mention of renting, or of landlords. Choice *C* is correct because Joseph Bruin bought hundreds of slaves during the years 1844 to 1861. Choice *D* is incorrect because the Bruin Slave Jail is stated as NOT open to the public. Choice *E* is incorrect because the passage notes that the offices and slave holding units were open until the end of the Civil War.

48. A: Choices *B*, *C*, *D*, and *E* can all be regarded as false based on the information provided in the passage. Choice *A* contains information provided in the passage; therefore, the statement is true. Choice *B* is false because the passage infers that Joseph Bruin was notorious as a slave trader; in fact, two sisters tried to run away from Joseph Bruin. Choice *C* is false because the slave pen was not four stories high; the passage specifically noted that the slave pen was two stories high. Choice *D* is false because the passage does not refer to Union or Confederate soldiers, and the Bruin Slave Jail was what became the Fairfax County courthouse. Choice *E* is false because there is no information in the passage that indicates that literature, like *Uncle Tom's Cabin*, was preserved by the Northern Virginia Urban League.

49. C: The purpose of the passage is to shed light on the history of Joseph Bruin's Slave Jail and what became of it. Choice *A* is incorrect because while the two sisters are mentioned in the story to provide details, they are not the main purpose of the story. Choice *B* is incorrect because while the beginning of the story contains the information about the town and its slave business, this answer option leaves out the fact that the passage is focused on one slave jail in particular and omits anything about the conclusion of the passage, which is actually key in the main focus of the passage—how Joseph Bruin's Slave Jail came about and what became of it. Choice *D* is incorrect because the point of the passage is not about where the historical Bruin Slave Jail currently stands, but the history behind it.

50. C: Because the details in Choice *A* and Choice *B* are examples of how an emotionally intelligent leader operates, they are not the best choice for the definition of the term *emotional intelligence*. They are qualities observed in an EI leader. Choice *C* is true as noted in the second sentence of the passage: Emotional Intelligence (EI) includes developing the ability to know one's own emotions, to regulate impulses and emotions, and to use interpersonal communication skills with ease while dealing with other people. It makes sense that someone with well-developed emotional intelligence will have a good handle on understanding his or her emotions and be able to regulate impulses and emotions and use honed interpersonal communication skills. Choice *D* is not a definition of EI. Choice *E* is the opposite of the definition of EI, so both Choice *D* and Choice *E* are incorrect.

51. C: Choice *E* can be eliminated immediately because of the signal word "obviously." Choice *A* can be eliminated because it does not reflect an accurate fact. Choices *B* and *D* do not support claims about how to be a successful leader.

52. E: The qualities of an unsuccessful leader possessing a transactional leadership style are listed in the passage. Choices *A* and *B* are incorrect because these options reflect the qualities of a successful leader. Choices *C* and *D* are definitely not characteristics of a successful leader; however, they are not presented in the passage and readers should do their best to ignore such options.

53. D: Even though some choices may be true of successful leaders, the best answer must be supported by sub-points in the passage. Therefore, Choices *A* and *C* are incorrect. Choice *B* is incorrect because uncompromising transactional leadership styles squelch success. *Choice* E is never mentioned in the passage.

54. B: Readers should carefully focus their attention on the beginning of the passage to answer this series of questions. Even though the sentences may be worded a bit differently, all but one statement is true. It presents a false idea that descriptive details are not necessary until the climax of the story. Even if one does not read the passage, he or she probably knows that all good writing begins with descriptive details to develop the main theme the writer intends for the narrative.

55. B: To suggest that a ten-minute play is accessible does not imply any timeline, nor does the passage mention how long a playwright spends with revisions and rewrites. So, Choice *A* is incorrect. Choice *B* is correct because of the opening statement that reads, "Learning how to write a ten-minute play may seem like a monumental task at first; but, if you follow a simple creative writing strategy, similar to writing a narrative story, you will be able to write a successful drama." None of the remaining choices are supported by points in the passage.

56. E: Note that the only element not mentioned in the passage is the style feature that is part of a narrative writer's tool kit. It is not to say that ten-minute plays do not have style. The correct answer denotes only that the element of style was not illustrated in this particular passage.

57. C: This choice allows room for the fact that not all people who attempt to write a play will find it easy. If the writer follows the basic principles of narrative writing described in the passage, however, writing a play does not have to be an excruciating experience. None of the other options can be supported by points from the passage.

Improving Sentences

58. B: Choice *B* is correct. Here, a colon is used to introduce an explanation. Colons either introduce explanations or lists. Additionally, the quote ends with the punctuation inside the quotes, unlike Choice *C*.

59. D: The word *civilised* should be spelled *civilized.* The words "makes," "human," "distinguishes," and "creatures," are all spelled correctly.

60. A: Choice *A* is correct because the phrase "others' ideas" is both plural and indicates possession. Choice *B* is incorrect because "other's" indicates only one "other" that's in possession of "ideas," which is incorrect. Choice *C* is incorrect because no possession is indicated. Choice *D* is incorrect because the word "other" does not end in *s*. *Others's* is not a correct form of the plural possessive word. Choice *E* is incorrect, as there is no reason the word "others" should be in quotations.

61. D: This sentence must have a comma before "although" because the word "although" is connecting two independent clauses. Thus, Choices *B* and *C* are incorrect. Choice *A* is incorrect because the second sentence in the underlined section is a fragment. Choice *E* is incorrect. Ellipses (. . .) are used to indicate an omitted phrase.

62. C: Choice *C* is the correct choice because the word "their" indicates possession, and the text is talking about "their students," or the students of someone. Choice *A*, "there," means at a certain place and is incorrect. Choice *B*, "they're," is a contraction and means "they are." Choices *D* and *E* are incorrect because these contain a singular pronoun, and our noun, "teachers," is plural.

63. B: Choice *B* uses all punctuation correctly in this sentence. In American English, single quotes should only be used if they are quotes within a quote, making Choices *A* and *C* incorrect. Additionally, punctuation should go inside the quotation marks with a few exceptions, making Choice *D* incorrect. Choice *E* is incorrect; the "why" should be in some sort of quotes since it is a questioning term within the sentence.

64. A: Choice *A* has consistent parallel structure with the verbs "read," "identify," and "determine." Choices *B* and *C* have faulty parallel structure with the words "determining" and "identifying." Choice *D* has incorrect subject/verb agreement. The sentence should read, "Students have to read . . . identify . . . and determine." Choice *E* is incorrect; the word "reading" should be "read."

65. D: Choice *D* uses the correct punctuation. American English uses double quotes unless placing quotes within a quote (which would then require single quotes). Thus, Choices *A* and *C* are incorrect. Choice *B* is incorrect because the period should go outside of the parenthesis, not inside. Choice *E* is incorrect; parenthesis around "wretched ones" causes the sentence to have problems. A sentence should be able to stand on its own without the words in the parenthesis completing it.

First Essay

Prepare an essay of about 300-600 words on the topic below.

Some people feel that sharing their lives on social media sites such as Facebook, Instagram, and Snapchat is fine. They share every aspect of their lives, including pictures of themselves and their families, what they ate for lunch, who they are dating, and when they are going on vacation. They even say that if it's not on social media, it didn't happen. Other people believe that sharing so much personal information is an invasion of privacy and could prove dangerous. They think sharing personal pictures and details invites predators, cyberbullying, and identity theft.

Write an essay to someone who is considering whether to participate in social media. Take a side on the issue and argue whether or not he/she should join a social media network. Use specific examples to support your argument.

Second Essay

Read the two articles below. Then, write a 500-word essay in which you synthesize the two articles with your own opinion of the topic. That is, you must develop a position of the topic then use both sources to draw upon your knowledge of the topic and appeal to your audience. Refer to each source by the author's last name or title.

Excerpt from *Preface to Lyrical Ballads* by William Wordsworth (1800)

From such verses the Poems in these volumes will be found distinguished at least by one mark of difference, that each of them has a worthy *purpose.* Not that I always began to write with a distinct purpose formerly conceived; but habits of meditation have, I trust, so prompted and regulated my feelings, that my descriptions of such objects as strongly excite those feelings, will be found to carry along with them a *purpose.* If this opinion be erroneous, I can have little right to the name of a Poet. For all good poetry is the spontaneous overflow of powerful feelings: and though this be true, Poems to which any value can be attached were never produced on any variety of subjects but by a man who, being possessed of more than usual organic sensibility, had also thought long and deeply. For our continued influxes of feeling are modified and directed by our thoughts, which are indeed the representatives of all our past feelings; and, as by contemplating the relation of these general representatives to each other, we discover what is really important to men, so, by the repetition and continuance of this act, our feelings will be connected with important subjects, till at length, if we be originally possessed of much sensibility, such habits of mind will be produced, that, by obeying blindly and mechanically the impulses of those habits, we shall describe objects, and utter sentiments, of such a nature, and in such connexion with each other, that the understanding of the Reader must necessarily be in some degree enlightened, and his affections strengthened and purified.

Excerpt from *Tradition and the Individual Talent* by T.S. Eliot (1921)

If you compare several representative passages of the greatest poetry you see how great is the variety of types of combination, and also how completely any semi-ethical criterion of "sublimity" misses the mark. For it is not the "greatness," the intensity, of the emotions, the components, but the intensity of the artistic process, the pressure, so to speak, under which the fusion takes place, that counts. The episode of Paolo and Francesca employs a definite emotion, but the intensity of the poetry is something quite different from whatever intensity in the supposed experience it may give the impression of. It is no more intense, furthermore, than Canto XXVI, the voyage of Ulysses, which has not the direct dependence upon an emotion. Great variety is possible in the process of transmution of emotion: the murder of Agamemnon, or the agony of Othello, gives an artistic effect apparently closer to a possible original than the scenes from Dante. In the *Agamemnon,* the artistic emotion approximates to the emotion of an actual spectator; in *Othello* to the emotion of the protagonist himself. But the difference between art and the event is always absolute; the combination which is the murder of Agamemnon is probably as complex as that which is the voyage of Ulysses. In either case there has been a fusion of elements. The ode of Keats contains a number of feelings which have nothing particular to do with the nightingale, but which the nightingale, partly, perhaps, because of its attractive name, and partly because of its reputation, served to bring together.

Dear CLEP College Composition Test Taker,

We would like to start by thanking you for purchasing this study guide for your CLEP College Composition exam. We hope that we exceeded your expectations.

Our goal in creating this study guide was to cover all of the topics that you will see on the test. We also strove to make our practice questions as similar as possible to what you will encounter on test day. With that being said, if you found something that you feel was not up to your standards, please send us an email and let us know.

We would also like to let you know about other books in our catalog that may interest you.

AP Biology

This can be found on Amazon: amazon.com/dp/1628456221

AP Comparative Government and Politics

amazon.com/dp/1628453230

GRE

amazon.com/dp/162845900X

SAT

amazon.com/dp/1628456868

ACT

amazon.com/dp/1628459468

We have study guides in a wide variety of fields. If the one you are looking for isn't listed above, then try searching for it on Amazon or send us an email.

Thanks Again and Happy Testing!
Product Development Team
info@studyguideteam.com

FREE Test Taking Tips DVD Offer

To help us better serve you, we have developed a Test Taking Tips DVD that we would like to give you for FREE. **This DVD covers world-class test taking tips that you can use to be even more successful when you are taking your test.**

All that we ask is that you email us your feedback about your study guide. Please let us know what you thought about it – whether that is good, bad or indifferent.

To get your **FREE Test Taking Tips DVD**, email freedvd@studyguideteam.com with "FREE DVD" in the subject line and the following information in the body of the email:

a. The title of your study guide.

b. Your product rating on a scale of 1-5, with 5 being the highest rating.

c. Your feedback about the study guide. What did you think of it?

d. Your full name and shipping address to send your free DVD.

If you have any questions or concerns, please don't hesitate to contact us at freedvd@studyguideteam.com.

Thanks again!

Made in United States
Troutdale, OR
01/24/2024

17107806R10073